Once Five Years Pass

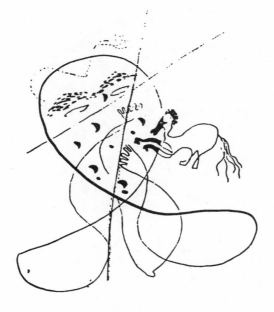

Federico García
LORCA

Once Five Years Pass
and other dramatic works

translated by **William Bryant Logan & Angel Gil Orrios**

foreword by Christopher Maurer

C 1

Station Hill Press

Library of Congress Cataloging-in-Publication Data

García Lorca, Federico, 1989-1936.
[Plays. English. Selections]
Once five years pass and other dramatic works / Federico García Lorca: translated by William Bryant Logan & Angel Gil Orrios.
p. cm.
ISBN 0-88268-070-6
1. García Lorca, Federico, 1898-1936—Translations, English.
I. Logan, William Bryant. II. Gil Orrios, Angel. III. Title.
PQ6613.A763A6 1989
862'.62—dc19

Manufactured in the United States of America.

For Susan and Soledad

Contents

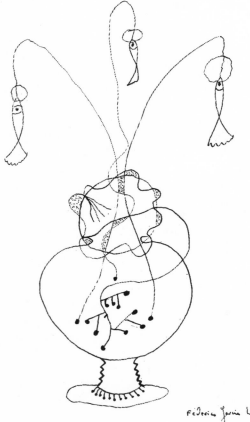

Jarrón de los tres peces [1935–1936]

Vase of the Three Fish

List of Illustrations

The Drawings of Federico García Lorca

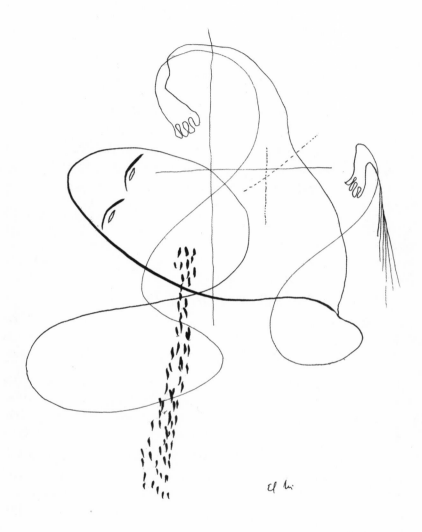

El hi (?) [h. 1929–1931]

The Son (?)...

Foreword

Fifty years after his death, Federico García Lorca is remembered, as a playwright, for three tragedies set in rural Spain: *Blood Wedding*, *Yerma* and *The House of Bernarda Alba*. This rural trilogy has drawn attention away from "another" Lorca, the author of less conventional works like *The Audience* and, in a very different vein, *Once Five Years Pass*.

Toward the end of his life, García Lorca hinted that his true direction in the theatre lay not in the rural dramas which had brought him renown, but in these two plays, which he had begun in New York and Havana (1929–30). "My true purpose [*mi verdadero propósito*] lies in these 'impossible plays,'" he remarks in an interview in 1936. "But in order to establish my personality and to win respect, I have written other things." Whether or not *Once Five Years Pass* reveals a more "authentic" Lorca than, say, *Blood Wedding* is debatable. But clearly there is in the former a larger measure of rebellion against the restraints and conventions of the commercial theatre. Lorca's first reference to this play seems to occur in a letter to his family (New York, 21 October 1929): "I have begun to write a play which might prove interesting. We must think of the theatre of tomorrow. All that now exists in Spain is dead. We either change the theatre completely or it will die away forever. There is no other solution."

A word must be said about the novelty and importance of this translation. Lorca's characters, especially those of the rural dramas, have never spoken English very convincingly. Reviewers of a version of *Blood Wedding* performed during Lorca's lifetime at the Neighborhood Playhouse, New York, complained of the "waxy flowers of speech," of characters relentlessly "talking poetic symbolism." One writer found it "difficult to retain composure while a widowed mother laments the violent passing of her husband and her first-born and remarks broodingly, 'My men were like two geraniums.'" Another wrote: "If the click of the castanets, the swish of the mantilla and the heavy roll of Andalusian rhetoric is music to your ears, here is a concert."

The importance of this translation is two-fold. Not only have William Logan and Angel Gil drawn attention to an unjustly neglected current of Lorca's theatre; they have also rid his characters of their foreign accent. They have avoided semi-literal translation ("And what is happening with you, my little son?") and "foreign flavor."

Once Five Years Pass was not performed during Lorca's lifetime, and its text has until now remained in ruins. Over the past several years, Gil and Logan have interviewed members of the amateur theatrical group (Club Anfistora) that was to have put on the play in 1936, under Lorca's direction, and have collated actors' scripts with published versions and the autograph manuscript. The translation published here is thus based on a new Spanish text which emends numerous scribal errors and brings to light small but destructive acts of censorship committed in previous versions. It is an admirable anniversary tribute, an attempt to restore and justly interpret García Lorca's dream of time, and dream of timeless theatre.

Christopher Maurer

Acknowledgements

The translators gratefully acknowledge the Theatre Communications Group who commissioned these translations of *Once Five Years Pass*. Special thanks to Christopher Maurer, James Leverett, Felix Navarro, and Santiago Ontañon for all their help and advice. Thanks too to the assemblage of talented actors and friends whose read-through of the first draft of *Once Five Years Pass* helped us to make important improvements in the translation. And finally, we are very grateful to George Quasha of Station Hill Press who agreed to publish these translations and to the grace and persistence of managing editor Juliana Spahr.

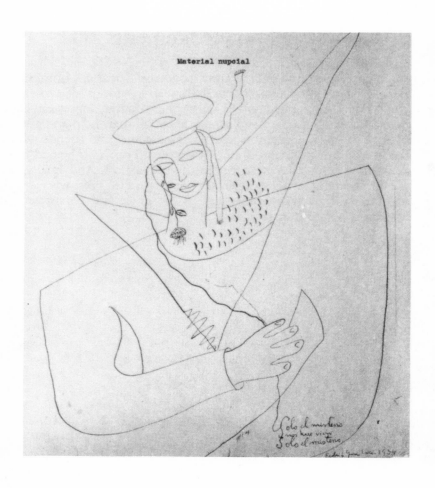

«Material nupcial»

Nuptial Material

Introduction

Once Five Years Pass is both the most intimate and most ambitious play by Federico García Lorca (1898–1936), the Spanish poet and playwright whose impact on world poetry and theater has been immense. Begun in New York in 1929 and finished in Lorca's home town of Granada on August 19, 1931, it is the fruit of his quest to write the "theatre of tomorrow." (Strangely, he was shot to death near Granada on August 19, 1936, once precisely five years had passed.) Though it was condensed into a ballet (with music by Paul Bowles, for Merce Cunningham) in 1943 and was a great success as a radio play in France, only now is the theatre coming to claim this remarkable synthetic work for its own.

Lorca has always been better known for his rural tragedies—*Blood Wedding*, *Yerma*, and *The House of Bernarda Alba*—but in April 1936, he himself judged these works less important to his "real purpose" than his "impossible plays," *Once Five Years Pass*, *The Audience*, and *Play without a Title*. What was his purpose? "We either change the theatre completely, or it will die forever," he wrote in a letter from New York to his family. "There is no other solution."

Once Five Years Pass was Lorca's favorite play and among his first mature works, the result of more than a decade's experiments (many of which are still unpublished!). It was, by his own assessment, a more essential work than the three rural tragedies, which he said were written "in order to establish my personality and to win respect." Only today, more than 50 years later, has there arisen a total theatre that synthesizes poetry, drama, music, and dance as successfully as did Lorca in *Once Five Years Pass*.

The plot outline is as archetypal as a fairy tale's: A Young Man goes to claim his young bride. He had agreed to wait five years to marry her, and at last the time is up. He arrives at her house only to find that she has just eloped with a large and brutal Football Player, who does nothing but squeeze her and blow cigar smoke in her face. Heartbroken, the Young Man wanders home through a forest and a circus, taunted on his way by a Clown, a Harlequin and a girl (his Typist) whom he had earlier rejected. In the end, Three Cardplayers come to play the Young Man for his Ace . . . his Ace of Hearts, and, when they have forced him to show the card, they shoot it (and the Young Man) down.

Given the intervention of the Clown and Harlequin, it is easy to see how the plot reflects the conventions of commedia dell-arte and of the puppet theatre: the Young Man is, strictly speaking, a Pierrot figure, constantly mis-advised and betrayed. But as his tragicomedy is worked out, it acquires elements of the silent film, the ballet, the art song, and especially the medieval mystery theatre.

Lorca himself once called the work "a mystery play about time, in prose and verse." The structure is circular, beginning and ending in the Young Man's library. Echoes double voices and clock chimes, but it is clear that no time has passed during the entire course of the play's action, making all that has transpired take on the character of the Young Man's dream. All the incidental characters—the Old Man, the Friends, the Boy and Cat, the Mannequin—can be seen as projections of the Young Man's emotional state.

Essentially this same symbolic characterization and preoccupation with time occur in the great 17th-century allegorical *autos sacramentales* of the Redemption, written by Lorca's favorite, Pedro Calderón de la Barca. The Young Man falls from the grace of his youth, becoming "exposed to the wind and death," as the Old Man puts it. His idealized Love, the Fiancée, betrays him cavalierly, leaving him lost in the forest from which only some new sort of Love might rescue him. The case is the same in Calderón's allegorical version of *Life is a Dream*, where Man pursues the faithless Shadow, only to be saved beyond hope by Christ's real Love. The difficulty for Lorca is that there is no saving Grace for his Young Man; his search for Real Love leads him round in circles of time, beginning in hope and ending in a losing card game.

Sources

Once Five Years Pass is not, as some critics have portrayed it, a surrealist work. It is a dream autobiography, with roots in the poet's own deep past. Subtitled "Legend of Time," it is the single work in which Lorca brings to fruition more than a decade of personal poems about the frustration of fruitless love, the loss of youth and the certainty of death. It is close in tone to what Lorca called, in a letter sending two poems to his friend Sebastian Gasch in 1928, "my new spiritual manner, pure lean emotion, loosed from logical control, but—careful!, careful!—with a tremendous poetic logic." And the poet continued, "It isn't surrealism—careful!—the purest consciousness illuminates [the poems]."

According to Isabel García Lorca, the poet's sister, the ultimate sources of the play are to be found directly in Lorca's childhood. In an interview with Marcelle Auclair, she declared that the work was "entirely made of my brother's childhood memories, scarcely transposed. Thus, the Clown of Act Three is the little boy who came to play with us in a clown costume. The episode of the cat's death and that of the boy's burial are practically the same as the real experiences. And so many more. . . ."[1]

Lorca's early poems became a mine of material for *Once Five Years Pass*. The seed of the whole play can be found in "Leyenda a medio abrir" (Half-Open Legend), a poem written in June 1918, when Lorca was but 20 years old, and only published in 1986, by Eutimio Martin in *F.G.L., heterodoxo y martir*.[2] The poem itself is homage to "La Légende du beau Pecopin et de la belle Bauldour," Chapter XXI of Victor Hugo's book of tales, *Le Rhin*. In the "Légende," the young Pecopin, having spent five years on a journey away from his betrothed, Bauldour, is lured into a forest ("the forest of lost paths") by the devil, just before he returns to claim her. Pecopin agrees to the devil's insistence that they spend one night hunting together, but the night lasts 100 years, so that when Pecopin at last appears before his beloved, she is a hideous old crone, and he, tearing off the talisman that had preserved his own youth, instantly grows a century older.

The Hugo tale was an obsession with Lorca, whose brother Francisco reported that the two of them used to play a game with it. Speaking of their life in 1910, when the poet was just entering puberty, Francisco wrote, "We shared the same room. Federico was never able to fall asleep without reading. . . . But I couldn't fall asleep with the light on. . . . Finally, we agreed that Federico would read on every other night, but Federico made me promise that before turning out the light, we would recite the following dialogue:

Federico: Pecopin, Pecopin.
Me: Baldour, Baldour.
Federico: Turn off, turn off
Me: The light, the light.

Only then would he put out the light without reading."[3]

Eutimio Martin has shown that Lorca's "Leyenda a medio abrir"
(Half-Open Legend)—whose title itself echoes the subtitle of *Once
Five Years Pass*, "Leyenda del tiempo" ("Legend of Time")—contains in embryo the premises and imagery of the play. (See our
translation in Appendix 1.) In the poem, the poet retells the Hugo
story, emphasizing the passage of time, and inserting himself as the
young (joven) poet, without a lover, afraid that overnight he could
die of an old (viejo) heart.

Of the same period are Lorca's first efforts to deal with fruitless
love as a condition of his homosexuality. In the still unpublished
"Pierrot (poema intimo)" (1918), the title character says, "Oh,
what a sadness of physiology!" and continues, "I had in my soul a
vague legend of woman." The outcome is this: "An exotic and
distant virgin and a muscular man of steel dance in me. My heart
does not know what to do." Here, a commedia dell'arte figure
assumes much the same role as the Young Man of *Once Five Years
Pass*, who will play Pierrot to the vicious Clown and Harlequin.

The same thematic material is developed further in the *Suites*,
written between 1921 and 1923, but only published in 1983 (in
an edition by Andre Belamich[4]). In these remarkable poems—de-
scriptions of a journey through time—Lorca works a Calderonian
magic on the unity of character and the sequence of events: He
multiplies the poetic "I" into different personae, causes echoes in
time, and writes the tragedy not simply of loss, but of what might-
have-been-but-never-was. In a letter about the poems written in
1923 to his friend Melchor Fernandez Almagro, he was more spe-
cific about the question of missed chances: "the garden of that
which is not but could have (and sometimes ought to have) been;
the garden of the theories that passed unperceived and of the children who were never born."

Many of the *Suites* contain material that was later reworked in
Once Five Years Pass: two of the songs are drawn from "El regreso"
("The Return") and from "Cuco-cuco-cuco" ("Cuckoo-Cuckoo-
Cuckoo"), and echoes in time occur in "La selva de los relojes"

("The Forest of the Clocks"). But the most telling material comes from the successive drafts "El jardin de las toronjas de luna" and "El bosque de las toronjas de luna" ("The Garden/The Forest of the Grapefruits of Moon"). The former converts the poet into a trio, "I/you/he (on a single plane)," whose characters converse among themselves. Appendix 2 contains our translation of the Prologue of the latter, in which the poet speaks of departing on a "long journey" that begins with his looking in the mirror.

One other work of the same period as the *Suites* contains the first clear theatrical allusion to what would become *Once Five Years Pass*. In *Los titeres de cachiporra* (1922), a puppet play, a character named "El Joven" (The Young Man) remarks "She loved me so . . . ," and another character adds, "five years ago."

What brought all of these threads of memory, poetry and drama together into *Once Five Years Pass*? Two events in the late 1920s focused the issues in Lorca's own life. The first was a simple rite of passage: between 1918 and 1928, Lorca had lived as a student in Madrid's Residence de Estudiantes, the cradle of artists like himself, Luis Buñuel and Salvador Dalí. Then, at the age of 30, he was forced for the first time into the world as an adult.

At almost the same time, he suffered a crisis in his love life, involving a break-up with the young sculptor Emilio Aladrén. Eight years Lorca's junior, Aladrén was an extraordinarily handsome young man. The two had met in 1925, and they were inseparable between 1927 and 1929, when the sculptor suddenly left Lorca to marry a woman. It was then that the broken-hearted Lorca decided to make a trip to New York, where he would begin to write *Once Five Years Pass*.

Synthesis

New York represented more than a refuge for Lorca. When he returned to Spain in 1931, he had undergone a change. As his friend, the poet Luis Cernuda, recalled, "I seemed to note a greater decisiveness in his attitude, as if something once intimate and secret in him had been affirmed." Four years later, the Lorca who had left for New York with one popular book of Andalusian poetry to his credit, had become the leading playwright of his generation, the accomplished director of the experimental theatre "La Barraca," and a remarkable poet in the Spanish baroque tradition.

In one of his last interviews, on November 15, 1935, Lorca

defined his own project for the theatre: "The root of my theatre is Calderonian. Magic theatre." Like Calderón, Lorca evolved a dual program of realist and symbolic theatre, mixing symbolic elements into the realist and vice versa. As Calderón had his "comedias" and "autos sacramentales," so Lorca has his rural plays and his "impossible theatre."

This theatrical vocation was confirmed during Lorca's time in New York. As he later wrote, "The new theatre, advanced in form and theory, is my greatest interest. New York is a matchless place to take the pulse of the new theatrical art." No one knows exactly what he saw there, but as Christopher Maurer has suggested[5], it is probable that he became familiar with the then very lively experimental theatres of the Neighborhood Playhouse, the Theatre Guild and the Civic Repertory Theatre. The first of these, particularly, was at that time experimenting with inter-generic collaborations, including dance, symphonic music and folk song in its 1929–30 theatre productions. Then too, as Maurer points out, Lorca certainly saw Black music-hall revues in Harlem—of which the poet wrote eloquently—and kept postcards showing characters from the archetypal theatres of China and Tibet.

Nevertheless, when he went to New York in 1929, Lorca already had more than a decade of dramatic experiments behind him. Among the earliest were the still unpublished five *Estados sentimentales* (*Emotional Moods*) and several *Místicas* (*Mysticals*), two series of contemplative interior monologues and dialogues begun in 1917. Though they were not intended for the stage, they included genuine dialogue, such as the conversation between a young man and the devil in "Encuentro"(1922).

At the same time, he wrote a number of allegorical dialogues (unpublished). In reality, they are his first theatrical works. Two versions of a work called *Cristo* date from 1917 or 1918. *Sombras* (*Shadows*), a work of 1920, has as characters, the shadows of Socrates, a Boy, and a Gardener, along with 6 unnamed shadows. A burlesque dialogue, *Jehova*, dates from the same year. According to his brother Francisco, Lorca was then reading the Spanish mystics together with books on Indian religion, but here too we can see at least the roots of the playwright's interest in the allegorical theatre of Calderón, an interest that would lead him to stage Calderón's *auto*, *La vida es sueño* (*Life Is a Dream*) as the premiere production of his travelling theatre company, La Barraca, in 1932.

Much of the unpublished early work is of interest for the understanding of *Once Five Years Pass*. As early as 1917, in "Fray Antonio (poema raro)" ["Brother Antonio (Strange Poem)"], Lorca sketches a character who can never possess one woman because he loves them all, a clear antecedent of the First Friend of *Once Five Years Pass*. Around the same time, he had also written six "cantos" of a work called "Historia vulgar" ("Plain History"), in which a young man dies of a broken heart when his girl emigrates to Buenos Aires.

Perhaps of greatest interest is the "Sonata que es una fantasía" ("Sonata That Is a Fantasia"), an early prose work written in a specified musical form. The subject matter is a dialogue among instruments concerning the lost love of the protagonist—the violin and the trumpets of *Once Five Years Pass* appear here too; but the form—depending on statements of theme, variation of speed and tone—are also structurally reminiscent of *Once Five Years Pass*.

> "*Primer tiempo*: Minuetto con variazioni [en] sol mayor
> Tema
> primera variacion
> segunda variacion
> tercera variacion
> *Segundo tiempo*: Allegro doloroso
> [*Tercer tiempo*]: Presto
> *Cuarto tiempo*: Andante tranquilo
> Coda"[6]

Lorca, who was an accomplished pianist and a friend of Manuel de Falla, was fascinated by the idea of giving musical form to drama and poetry. In the structure of the above sonata, one senses the same attention to rhythm and tone that would inform *Once Five Years Pass*.

The relationship between music and drama is even more clearly revealed in the early "Sonata de la nostalgia" ("Sonata of Nostalgia"), where a young man complains to his beloved, with piano accompaniment:

> "My soul is overflowing with passion. Why don't you love me? Why are you leaving me . . . ? Where will you go . . . ?
> *Adagio cantabile* (firmly)
> I'm going to the light, to the truth. Don't ask me more. It's senseless. I don't love you anymore.
> *Molto allegro con fuoco*

Acordes de dominante
My God. She was my dream. Why is she leaving me?"

The whole dramatic emotional structure of *Once Five Years Pass* is a fuller version of this early sketch.

A further step in the technical evolution that would culminate in *Once Five Years Pass* are the short dialogues of 1925–1926 and the filmscript of 1930, which we have translated as part of this volume. In all of these, Lorca works on a synthesis of poetry, film and theatrical technique. Not only in the filmscript *Viaje a la Luna* (*Trip to the Moon*) and in the dialogue *El Paseo de Buster Keaton* (*Buster Keaton's Outing*), but in the remaining dialogues, the changes of scene and the flow of events have the character of cinematic "cuts," like the juxtaposition of the scenes of the Dead Boy and the Dead Cat and of the Mannequin in *Once Five Years Pass*. In these short works, too, Lorca experiments with "impossible" stage directions that bring some part of the scenery alive, just as the Mannequin will come to life and as the Ace of Hearts will be projected on the wall and shot by the Cardplayers in *Once Five Years Pass*.

Among all the currents that meet in *Once Five Years Pass*, however, perhaps none is so strong as the dichotomy that Lorca first broached in his 1926 lecture, "The Poetic Image of Don Luis de Góngora"—revised for presentation in New York in 1930, just at the time he was writing the play—between "people who make their poems as they walk the roads versus people who make their poems seated at the table, watching the roads through the leaded panes of the window." This is precisely the quandary in which the Young Man finds himself during Act One, as he attempts to shut out the noises of the street and also to ignore any facts about his beloved that might not accord with his image of her. The Old Man encourages the Young Man's isolation, even suggesting that he conceal the passing of time by renaming years as "snows," "sunsets," "skies," much as the poet Góngora himself had done in the rich baroque metaphorics of the *Soledades*.

At the same time, however, *Once Five Years Pass* is an extension of the pure (as opposed to popular) poetic impulse towards symbolic and metaphoric echoes. Just as he praised Góngora for "doubling and tripling the image to carry us off to different levels where he can perfect the sensation and connect it with all its other aspects," so in the play, Lorca replicates the Young Man in time as Old Man (future), First Friend (present), and Second Friend (past), and these characters themselves are further multiplied in other minor characters. (For this reason, the play can be performed with many fewer actors than the 21 roles suggest.)

Furthermore, what is true for the poet of Lorca's Góngora lecture is true for the Young Man: "The poet who is about to make a poem . . . has the vague feeling he is going on a nocturnal hunting trip in an incredibly distant forest. An inexplicable fear murmurs in his heart. . . . One must set out, and this is the dangerous moment for the poet. . . . " When the Young Man leaves his house to claim his Fiancée, and later when he wanders in the Forest, this is exactly the trip he takes.

The Young Man is a poet like Lorca's Góngora, but with a difference. The whole work may be said to take place as a revery inside the Young Man's head. "One returns from inspiration as one returns from a foreign country," Lorca had written in the Góngora lecture, "The poem is the narration of the trip." So, *Once Five Years Pass* is the dramatization of a psychological journey. But the Young Man has taken a risk that the poet Góngora did not: he has "exposed himself to the wind and death" and to the intimate conflict that threatens to destroy him.

Once Five Years Pass is a rite of passage for Lorca, and it is an astonishingly rich and challenging play. Some have said that it is an obscure work. One could instead say of it what Lorca says of Góngora's *Soledades*: "What is all this about obscurity? I think his sin was lucidity. But to reach him one must be initiated into poetry; one's sensibility must be prepared by reading and metaphorical experiences. Whoever is outside his world cannot savor it, just as he does not savor a picture though he sees what is painted in it, or a musical composition."

Arlequín desdoblado [1927]

Double Harlequin

Payaso de rostro desdoblado [1927]

Clown with Double Face

Así Que Pasen Cinco Años
Once Five Years Pass

Así Que Pasen Cinco Años
(Leyenda del Tiempo)[1]

Acto Primero

Biblioteca. EL JOVEN está sentado. Viste un pijama azul. EL VIEJO, de chaqué gris, con barba blanca y enormes lentes de oro, también sentado.

JOVEN

No me sorprende.[4]

VIEJO

Perdone . . .

JOVEN

Siempre me ha pasado igual.

VIEJO

[Inquisitivo y amable] ¿Verdad?

Once Five Years Pass
(Legend of Time)

Characters

YOUNG MAN	THE MANNEQUIN IN THE
OLD MAN	WEDDING DRESS
A DEAD BOY	THE FOOTBALL PLAYER
A DEAD CAT	THE MAID
SERVANT	THE FATHER OF THE FIANCÉE
FIRST FRIEND	CLOWN
SECOND FRIEND	HARLEQUIN
THE TYPIST	GIRL
THE FIANCÉE	MASKS AND CARDPLAYERS

Act One

Library. The YOUNG MAN is seated, wearing blue pajamas. The OLD MAN, in a gray cutaway coat, with a white beard and huge golden spectacles, also seated.

YOUNG MAN

I'm not surprised.

OLD MAN

Excuse me . . . .

YOUNG MAN

It's always been the same with me.

OLD MAN

[Inquisitive and friendly] Truly?

JOVEN

Sí.

VIEJO

Es que . . .

JOVEN

Recuerdo que . . .

VIEJO

[Ríe] Siempre recuerdo.

JOVEN

Yo . . .

VIEJO

[Anhelante] Siga . . .

JOVEN

Guardaba los dulces para comerlos después.

VIEJO

Después ¿verdad? Saben mejor. Yo también . . .

JOVEN

Y recuerdo que un día . . .

VIEJO

[Interrumpiendo con vehemencia] Me gusta tanto la palabra recuerdo. Es una palabra verde, jugosa. Mana sin cesar hilitos de agua fría.[5]

JOVEN

[Alegre y tratando de convencerse] Sí, sí ¡claro! Tiene usted razón.[6] Es preciso luchar con toda idea de ruinas; con esos terribles desconchados de las paredes. Muchas veces yo me he levantado a medianoche para arrancar las hierbas del jardín. No quiero hierbas en mi casa, ni muebles rotos.

YOUNG MAN

Yes.

OLD MAN

It's just that . . . .

YOUNG MAN

I remember . . . .

OLD MAN

[Laughs] Always, "I remember."

YOUNG MAN

I . . . .

OLD MAN

[Eager] Go on . . . .

YOUNG MAN

I used to save sweets to eat them later.

OLD MAN

Later they taste better, don't they? I, too . . . .

YOUNG MAN

And I remember one day . . . .

OLD MAN

[Interrupting vehemently] How I love the word remember. Such a green and succulent word.

YOUNG MAN

[Brightly and trying to convince himself] Yes, yes, of course! You're right. One must resist the very idea of decay . . . those terrible flakes of plaster on the walls. I get up all the time in the middle of the night just to rip the weeds out of the garden. I won't have weeds in this house, or broken furniture.

VIEJO

¡Eso! Ni muebles rotos, porque hay que recordar, pero . . .

JOVEN

Pero las cosas vivas, ardiendo en su sangre, con todos sus perfiles intactos.

VIEJO

¡Muy bien! Es decir . . . *[bajando la voz]* hay que recordar . . . pero recordar antes.

JOVEN

¿Antes?

VIEJO

[Con sigilo] Sí. Hay que recordar hacia mañana.

JOVEN

[Absorto] ¡Hacia mañana!

> *[Un reloj da las seis. LA MECANOGRAFA cruza la escena, llorando en silencio.]*

VIEJO

Las seis.

JOVEN

Sí, las seis y con demasiado calor. *[Se levanta]* Hay un cielo de tormenta hermoso. Lleno de nubes grises.

VIEJO

¿De manera que usted? . . .[7]

JOVEN

[Abanicándose] Yo espero.[8]

VIEJO

¿Con valor?

OLD MAN

Precisely! Or broken furniture, because one must remember, but . . . .

YOUNG MAN

But only what's alive, its blood burning, perfect from every angle.

OLD MAN

Excellent! I mean . . . *[Lowering his voice]* one must remember . . . , but remember before.

YOUNG MAN

Before?

OLD MAN

[Secretively] Yes, one must remember into tomorrow.

YOUNG MAN

[Absorbed in thought] Into tomorrow!

> *[A clock strikes six. The TYPIST crosses the stage, crying silently.]*

OLD MAN

Six o'clock.

YOUNG MAN

Six o'clock, indeed, and still too hot. *[He rises.]* What a lovely storm sky. All those gray clouds.

OLD MAN

In other words, you . . . ?

YOUNG MAN

[Fanning himself] I wait.

OLD MAN

With confidence?

JOVEN[9]

Usted me conoce ya.

VIEJO

¿Vino el padre de ella?

JOVEN

Nunca.[10]

VIEJO

Yo fuí gran amigo de esa familia. Sobre todo del padre. Se ocupa de astronomía. *[Irónico]*[11] Está bien ¿eh? De astronomía. ¿Y ella?

JOVEN

La he conocido poco. Pero no importa. Yo creo que me quiere.

VIEJO

¡Seguro!

JOVEN

Se fueron a un largo viaje. Casi me alegré . . .[12] Las cosas requieren tiempo.

VIEJO

[Alegre] ¡Claro!

JOVEN

Sí, pero . . .

VIEJO

Pero qué . . .

JOVEN

Nada;[13] por ahora no puede ser . . . por causas que no son de explicar. Yo no me casaré con ella . . . [14] ¡hasta que pasen cinco años!

YOUNG MAN

You know me.

OLD MAN

Have you met her father?

YOUNG MAN

Never.

OLD MAN

I was a great friend of the family. Especially the father. He's interested in astronomy. *[Ironically]* Not bad, eh? Astronomy. What about her?

YOUNG MAN

I don't know much about her. But it doesn't matter. I believe she loves me.

OLD MAN

Surely!

YOUNG MAN

They went on a long trip. I was practically happy . . . . These things take time.

OLD MAN

[Brightly] Precisely!

YOUNG MAN

Yes, but . . . .

OLD MAN

But what . . . .

YOUNG MAN

Nothing; for now, it's just not possible . . . for reasons I can't explain. I won't marry her . . . until five years pass!

VIEJO

[Con alegría] ¡Muy bien!

JOVEN

[Serio] ¿Por qué dice muy bien?

VIEJO

Pues porque ... ¿Es bonito esto? *[Señalando la habitación.]*

JOVEN

No.

VIEJO

¿No le angustia la hora de la partida, los acontecimientos, lo que ha de llegar ahora mismo? ...

JOVEN

Sí, sí. No me hable de eso.[15]

VIEJO

¿Qué pasa en la calle?

JOVEN

Ruido, ruido siempre, polvo, calor, malos olores. Me molesta que las cosas[16] de la calle entren en mi casa. *[Un gemido largo se oye. Pausa.]* Juan: cierra la ventana.

> *[Un CRIADO sutil que anda sobre las puntas de los pies cierra el ventanal.]*

VIEJO

Ella ... es jovencita.[17]

JOVEN

Muy jovencita. ¡Quince años!

OLD MAN

[Brightly] Excellent!

YOUNG MAN

[Solemn] What makes it so excellent?

OLD MAN

Why, because . . . isn't this lovely? *[Pointing to the room]*

YOUNG MAN

No.

OLD MAN

Doesn't it make you miserable, the hour of parting, what could happen, what's about to occur right this minute . . . ?

YOUNG MAN

Yes, yes. I don't want to talk about it.

OLD MAN

What's happening on the street?

YOUNG MAN

Noise, noise and more noise, heat, dust, rotten smells. Why should I let these things from the street into my house? It bothers me. *[Sound of a prolonged wail. Pause.]* Juan, shut the window.

[An artful servant, walking on tiptoe, shuts the great window.]

OLD MAN

She's young?

YOUNG MAN

Very young. Fifteen years old!

VIEJO[18]

Quince años que ha vivido ella, que son ella misma. ¡Pero por qué no decir: tiene quince nieves, quince aires, quince crepúsculos! ¡No se atreve usted a huir!, ¡a volar!, ¡a ensanchar su amor por todo el cielo![19]

JOVEN

[Se sienta y[20] *se cubre la cara con las manos]* ¡La quiero demasiado!

VIEJO

[De pie y con energía] O bien decir: tiene quince rosas, quince alas, quince granitos de arena. ¡No se atreve usted a concentrar, a hacer hiriente y pequeñito su amor dentro del pecho![21]

JOVEN

Usted quiere apartarme de ella. [Pero ya conozco su procedimiento. Basta observar un rato sobre la palma de la mano un insecto vivo, o mirar al mar una tarde poniendo atención en la forma de cada ola, para que el rostro o la llaga que llevamos en el pecho se deshaga en burbujas.][22] Pero es que yo estoy enamorado y quiero estar enamorado, tan enamorado como ella lo está de mí, y por eso puedo aguardar[23] cinco años en espera de poder liarme de noche, con todo el mundo a oscuras,[24] sus trenzas de luz alrededor de mi cuello.

VIEJO

Me permito recordarle que su novia ... no tiene trenzas.

JOVEN

[Irritado] Ya lo sé. Se las cortó sin mi[25] permiso, naturalmente, y ésto ... *[con angustia]* me cambia su imagen. *[Enérgico]* ¡Ya sé que no tiene trenzas! *[Casi furioso]* ¿Por qué me lo ha recordado usted? *[Con tristeza]* Pero en estos cinco años las volverá a tener.

VIEJO

[Entusiasmado] Y más hermosas que nunca.[26] Serán unas trenzas ...

JOVEN

[Con alegría] Son, son.

OLD MAN

Fifteen years she's lived, and they are what she is. Why not say fifteen snows, fifteen winds, fifteen sunsets! You don't dare to run! To fly! To extend your love to the whole sky!

YOUNG MAN

[He sits down and covers his face with his hands.] I love her too much!

OLD MAN

[Standing and forcefully] You might as well say fifteen roses, fifteen wings, fifteen grains of sand. You don't dare to concentrate, to make your love little and painful in your heart!

YOUNG MAN

You want to keep me away from her. [I know how you operate. Just watch a live bug on the palm of your hand or spend an afternoon looking at the sea, paying attention to the shape of each wave, and the face or the sore we keep in our breast will simply dissolve in bubbles.]* But the thing is, I'm in love, and I want to be in love, as much in love with her as she with me. So I can bear five years, waiting for the night when while all the world's asleep, I can wind her shining braids around my neck.

OLD MAN

Permit me to remind you that your fiancée . . . hasn't got braids.

YOUNG MAN

[Irritated] I know that. She cut them without my permission, of course, and that . . . *[Miserably]* changes my picture of her. *[Emphatically]* I know she hasn't got braids! *[Practically infuriated]* Why do you have to remind me? *[Sadly]* Still, she has five years to grow them back.

OLD MAN

[Enthusiastically] And prettier than ever. What braids she'll have . . . .

YOUNG MAN

[Happily] Has now, has now.

---

*Bracketed by Lorca in manuscript for a possible cut.

VIEJO

[Condescendiente][27] Son unas trenzas con cuyo perfume se puede vivir sin necesidad de pan ni de agua.

JOVEN

[Se levanta][28] ¡Pienso tanto!

VIEJO

¡Sueña tanto!

JOVEN

¿Cómo?

VIEJO

Piensa tanto que . . .

JOVEN

Que estoy en carne viva. Todo hacia dentro una quemadura.[29]

VIEJO

[Alargándole un vaso][30] Beba.

JOVEN

¡Gracias! Si me pongo a pensar en la muchachita, en mi niña . . .

VIEJO

Diga usted: mi novia. ¡Atrévase!

JOVEN

No.

VIEJO

¿Pero por qué?

JOVEN

Novia . . . , ya lo sabe usted, si digo novia la veo sin querer amortajada en un cielo sujeto por enormes trenzas de nieve.[31] No, no es

OLD MAN

[Indulgent] She has such braids. Why, you could live on their perfume and never miss bread or water.

YOUNG MAN

[He rises] I think so much!

OLD MAN

You dream so much!

YOUNG MAN

What's that?

OLD MAN

You think so much that . . . .

YOUNG MAN

My flesh is raw. Burned inside.

OLD MAN

[Handing him a glass] Take a drink.

YOUNG MAN

Thank you! When I start thinking of my little girl, my child . . . .

OLD MAN

Try saying, my fiancée. Dare to!

YOUNG MAN

No.

OLD MAN

But why not?

YOUNG MAN

Fiancée . . . you know, as soon as I say fiancée I see her against my will shrouded in a sky tied up with great braids of snow. No, she mi novia, *[hace un gesto como si alejara*[32] *la imagen que quiere captarlo]* es mi niña, mi muchachita.[33] Pues si me pongo a pensar en ella . . .[34]

VIEJO

Siga, siga . . .

JOVEN

La dibujo, la hago moverse blanca y viva; pero de pronto ¿quién la cambia la nariz o la rompe los dientes o la convierte en otra, llena de andrajos, que va por mi pensamiento, monstruosa,[35] como si estuviera mirándose en un espejo de feria?

VIEJO

¿Quién? ¡Parece mentira que usted diga *quién!*[36] Todavía cambian más las cosas que tenemos delante de los ojos, que las que viven sin distancia[37] debajo de la frente. El agua que viene por el río es completamente distinta de la que se va.[38] Y ¿quién recuerda un mapa exacto de la arena del desierto . . . o del rostro de un amigo cualquiera?

JOVEN

Sí, sí. Aún está más vivo lo de adentro aunque también cambie. Mire usted;[39] la última vez que la ví no podía mirarla muy de cerca porque tenía dos arruguitas en la frente, que, como me descuidara . . . , ¿entiende usted?, la llenaban todo el rostro y la ponían ajada, vieja, como si hubiera sufrido mucho. Tenía necesidad de separarme para . . . ¡enfocarla!, ésta es la palabra, en mi corazón.

VIEJO

¿A que en aquel momento que la vió vieja, ella estaba completamente entregada a usted?

JOVEN

Sí.

VIEJO

¿Completamente dominada por usted?[40]

is not my fiancée, *[Making a gesture as though to push away an image that approaches him]* she's my child, my little girl. So if I start thinking of her . . . .

OLD MAN

Go on, go on . . . .

YOUNG MAN

I draw a picture of her, and I move her around, white and warm; then, all of a sudden, who is it changes her nose or breaks her teeth or turns her into somebody else, all in rags, monstrous, walking through my mind as though looking in a funhouse mirror?

OLD MAN

Who? I can't believe you ask *who*. And what's before our eyes changes even quicker than what lives at no distance beneath our foreheads. The water coming down the river is totally different from the water that flows on, and who remembers an exact map of the desert sands . . . or for that matter the face of a friend?

YOUNG MAN

Yes, yes. What's inside is more alive, though it changes too. For example, the last time I saw her, I could scarcely look at her because she had two little wrinkles on her forehead. If I'd blinked—you understand?—they could have covered her face and made her old and rumpled, as though she had suffered much. I had to keep my distance so as to . . . focus her—that's the word!—in my heart.

OLD MAN

Then the moment you saw her old, she was totally surrendered to you?

YOUNG MAN

Yes.

OLD MAN

Totally in your power?

JOVEN

Sí.

VIEJO

[*Exaltado*] ¿A que si en aquel preciso instante ella le confiesa que lo ha engañado, que no lo quiere, las arruguitas se le hubieran convertido[41] en la rosa más delicada del mundo?

JOVEN

[*Exaltado*] Sí.

VIEJO

¿Y la hubiera amado más precisamente por eso?

JOVEN

¡Sí, sí![42]

VIEJO

¿Entonces? ¡Ja, Ja, Ja!

JOVEN

Entonces... Es muy difícil vivir.

VIEJO

Por eso hay que volar de una cosa a otra hasta perderse. Si ella tiene quince años puede tener quince crepúsculos o quince cielos ¡y vamos arriba!, ¡a volar![43] Están las cosas más vivas dentro que ahí fuera, expuestas al aire o la muerte. Por eso; vamos a...a no ir...o a esperar. Porque lo otro es morirse *ahora mismo*[44] y es más hermoso pensar que, todavía mañana, veremos los cien cuernos de oro con que levanta a las nubes el sol.

JOVEN

[*Dándole la mano*] ¡Gracias! ¡Gracias por todo!

VIEJO

¡Volveré por aquí!

[*Aparece la MECANOGRAFA*]

YOUNG MAN

Yes.

OLD MAN

[Excited] So if at that very moment, she confesses that she's deceived you, that she doesn't really love you, those wrinkles would become the sweetest rose in the world?

YOUNG MAN

[Excited] Yes.

OLD MAN

And for just that reason, you'd have loved her all the more?

YOUNG MAN

Yes, yes!

OLD MAN

So? Ha, ha, ha!

YOUNG MAN

So . . . it's very hard to live.

OLD MAN

That's why you should fly from one thing to another until you're lost. If she's fifteen, she could as well be fifteen sunsets or fifteen skies. Onward and upward! Flying! What's inside is more alive than what's out there exposed to the wind and death. That's why; we are . . . not going to go . . . we are going to wait. Since the alternative is to die *right now* and it's prettier to think that we may still live to see the hundred horns of gold with which the sun wakes the clouds.

YOUNG MAN

[Taking his hand] Thank you! Thank you for everything!

OLD MAN

I'll be back again!

[The TYPIST appears.]

JOVEN

¿Terminó usted de escribir las cartas?

MECANOGRAFA

[*Llorosa*] Sí, señor.

VIEJO

[*Al JOVEN*] ¿Qué le ocurre?

MECANOGRAFA

Deseo marchar de esta casa.

VIEJO

Pues es bien fácil, ¿no?

JOVEN

[*Turbado*] ¡Verá usted . . . !

MECANOGRAFA

Quiero irme y no puedo.

JOVEN

[*Dulce*] No soy yo quien te retiene. Ya sabes que no puedo hacer nada. Te he dicho algunas veces que te esperaras, pero tú . . .

MECANOGRAFA

Pero yo no espero; ¡qué es eso de esperar!

VIEJO

[*Serio*] ¿Y por qué no? ¡Esperar es creer y vivir!

MECANOGRAFA

No espero porque no me da la gana, porque no quiero y, sin embargo, no me puedo mover de aquí.

YOUNG MAN

Have you finished writing the letters?

TYPIST

[*Tearfully*] Yes, sir.

OLD MAN

[*To the YOUNG MAN*] What's the matter with her?

TYPIST

I would like to leave this house.

OLD MAN

That's easily done, eh?

YOUNG MAN

[*Troubled*] You think so?

TYPIST

I want to and I can't.

YOUNG MAN

[*Sweetly*] I'm not the one that's keeping you. You know very well there's nothing I can do. I've asked you more than once to wait, but you . . . .

TYPIST

But I won't wait; what is all this waiting!

OLD MAN

[*Solemn*] Why ever not? To wait is to hope, to live and to believe!

TYPIST

I won't wait because I don't feel like it, because I don't want to, and still, I can't seem to get away from here.

JOVEN

¡Siempre acabas no dando razones!

MECANOGRAFA

¿Qué razones voy a dar? No hay más que una razón y esa es . . .
¡que te quiero! Desde siempre. *[Al VIEJO]* No se asombre usted.[45]
Cuando pequeñito yo lo veía jugar desde mi balcón. Un día se cayó
y sangraba por la rodilla, ¿te acuerdas? Todavía tengo aquella
sangre viva como una sierpe roja temblando[46] entre mis pechos.

VIEJO

Eso no está bien. La sangre se seca y lo pasado, pasado.

MECANOGRAFA

¡Qué culpa tengo yo, señor! *[Al JOVEN]* Yo te ruego me des la
cuenta. Quiero irme de esta casa.

JOVEN

[Irritado] Muy bien. Tampoco tengo yo culpa ninguna. Además,
sabes perfectamente que no me pertenezco. Puedes irte.

MECANOGRAFA

[Al VIEJO] ¿Lo ha oido usted? Me arroja de su casa. No quiere
tenerme aquí. *[Llora. Se va.]*

VIEJO

[Con sigilo al JOVEN] Es peligrosa esta mujer.

JOVEN

Yo quisiera quererla, como quisiera tener sed delante de las fuentes.
Quisiera.

VIEJO

De ninguna manera. ¿Qué haría usted mañana?, ¿eh? Piense.
¡Mañana!

YOUNG MAN

You get so irrational!

TYPIST

What reasons am I to give? There isn't but one reason, and that is...that I love you! I always have. *[To the OLD MAN]* Don't look so astonished. When he was little, I used to watch him playing from my balcony. One day he fell, and his knee bled, you remember? That bright blood still trembles like a red snake between my breasts.

OLD MAN

That's not right. Blood dries, and what's past is past.

TYPIST

Is that my fault, sir! *[To the YOUNG MAN]* Please pay me what you owe. I want to get out of this house.

YOUNG MAN

[Irritated] Very well. It's not my fault either. Besides, you know perfectly well that I belong to another. You may go.

TYPIST

[To the OLD MAN] Do you hear? He's throwing me out of his house. He doesn't want me here. *[She cries. She leaves.]*

OLD MAN

[Surreptitiously to the YOUNG MAN] That woman is dangerous.

YOUNG MAN

I'd love her if I only could, just as I'd love to be thirsty at a fountain. If I only could.

OLD MAN

By no means. Then what would you do tomorrow? Eh? Think about it. Tomorrow!

AMIGO

[Entrando con escándalo] ¡Cuánto silencio en esta casa! ¿Y para qué? Dáme agua. ¡Con anís y con hielo! *[El VIEJO se va.]* Un cock-tail.[47]

JOVEN

Supongo que no me romperás los muebles.

AMIGO

Hombre solo, hombre serio, ¡y con este calor!

JOVEN

¿No puedes sentarte?

AMIGO

[Lo coge en brazos y le da vueltas]
     Tin, tin, tan,
     la llamita de San Juan.

JOVEN

¡Déjame![48] No tengo ganas de bromas.

AMIGO

¡Mum! ¿Quién era ese viejo? ¿Un amigo tuyo? ¿Y dónde están en esta casa los retratos de las muchachas con las que tú te acuestas? Mira: *[se acerca]* te voy a coger de la solapa, te voy a pintar de colorete esas mejillas de cera . . . o así, restregadas.

JOVEN

[Irritado] ¡Déjame!

AMIGO[49]

Y con un bastón te voy a echar a la calle.

JOVEN

¿Y qué voy a hacer en ella? El gusto tuyo, ¿verdad? Demasiado trabajo tengo con oirla llena de coches y gentes desorientadas.

FRIEND

[Enters boisterously] Too quiet in this house! And what for? Water, please. With anise. On the rocks! *[The OLD MAN leaves.]* A *cocktail.*

YOUNG MAN

I hope you aren't going to break the furniture.

FRIEND

A man alone, a serious man, and in heat like this!

YOUNG MAN

Can't you sit down?

FRIEND

[Takes him by the arms and spins him around]
> ... And everywhere the monkey went,
> pop goes the weasel!

YOUNG MAN

Cut it out! I'm in no mood for jokes.

FRIEND

Uh oh! Who was that old man? A friend of yours? And where are the pictures in this house of the girls you sleep with? Look: *[Comes closer]* I'm going to grab you by the lapels, I'm going to smear rouge on those waxy cheeks of yours ..., or scrub them, like this.

YOUNG MAN

[Irritated] Cut it out!

FRIEND

And toss you out on the street with a cane.

YOUNG MAN

And what will I do there? Whatever you say, right? It's hard enough just listening to all the cars and milling crowds.

AMIGO

[Sentándose y estirándose en el sofá] ¡Ay! ¡Mum! Yo en cambio...
Ayer hice tres conquistas y como anteayer hice dos y hoy una, pues
resulta... que me quedo sin ninguna porque no tengo tiempo. Estuve con una muchacha... Ernestina. ¿La quieres conocer?

JOVEN

No.

AMIGO

[Levantándose] Nooo y rúbrica. ¡Pero si vieras! ¡Tiene un talle!...
No... aunque el talle lo tiene mucho mejor Matilde. *[Con ímpetu]*
¡Ay, Dios mío! *[Da un salto y cae tendido en el sofá]* Mira; es un talle
para la medida de todos los brazos y tan frágil que se desea tener
en la mano un hacha de plata muy pequeña para, zás,[50] seccionarlo.

JOVEN

[Distraído y aparte de la conversación] Entonces yo subiré la escalera.[51]

AMIGO

[Tendiéndose boca abajo en el sofá] ¡No tengo tiempo, no tengo tiempo
de nada! Todo se me atropella. Porque, ¡figúrate!, me cito con
Ernestina; los labios vueltos, *[se levanta]* las trenzas, aquí, apretadas,
negrísimas, y luego... Ernesti-ti-ti-ti-ti-ti-tina, tantas cosas dulces
le digo con su nombre que se le llenan los pechos de tes y, como le
hacen daño, se las tengo que ir quitando con los labios, con los
dedos, con los ojos...[52]

[El JOVEN golpea con impaciencia los dedos sobre la mesa.]

JOVEN

¡No me dejas pensar!

FRIEND

[Sitting down and stretching out on the sofa] Uh oh, uh oh! I on the other hand . . . with three conquests yesterday, two the day before and one today, I end up . . . with none at all because I have no time. I was with a girl . . . Ernestina. Want to meet her?

YOUNG MAN

No.

FRIEND

[Rising] No, period. If you only saw her! What a figure . . . ! No, Mathilde has a much nicer figure, but . . . . *[Impulsively]* My God! *[He jumps and falls full-length on the sofa]* Look; it's a figure made to order for every pair of arms and so delicate you want to have a tiny silver axe in your hand to—zas!—slice it up.

YOUNG MAN

[Distracted and apart from the conversation] Then I'll climb the stairs.

FRIEND

[Lying face down on the sofa] I have no time, no time for anything. It's all a blur. Because, just think of it, I make a date with Ernestina; lips so full *[Rises]* and braids down to here, tight and jet black, and then . . . Ernesti-ti-ti-ti-ti-ti-tina, I say such sweet things with her name alone that her tits are covered with T's, and since they hurt her, I have to take each of them off with my lips, with my fingers, with my eyes . . . .

> *[The YOUNG MAN impatiently drums on the table with his fingers.]*

YOUNG MAN

I can't think with you around!

AMIGO

¡Pero si no hay que pensar!⁵³ Y me voy. Por más...que... *[mira el reloj]* ya se ha pasado la hora. Es horrible, siempre ocurre igual. No tengo tiempo y lo siento. Iba con una mujer feísima, ¿lo oyes?, ja, ja, ja, ja, feísima,⁵⁴ pero adorable. Una morena de esas que se echan de menos al mediodía de verano,⁵⁵ y me gusta *[tira un cojín por alto]* porque parece un domador.

JOVEN

¡Basta!⁵⁶

AMIGO

Sí, hombre, no te indignes, pero una mujer puede ser feísima y un domador de caballos puede ser hermoso,⁵⁷ y al revés y... ¿qué sabemos? *[Llena una copa de cock-tail.]*

JOVEN

Nada...⁵⁸

AMIGO

¿Pero me quieres decir qué te pasa?

JOVEN

Nada.⁵⁹ ¿No me conoces? Es mi temperamento.⁶⁰

AMIGO

Yo no entiendo. No entiendo,⁶¹ pero tampoco puedo estar serio. *[Ríe]* Te saludaré como los chinos. *[Frota su nariz con la del JOVEN.]*

JOVEN

[Sonriendo] ¡Quita!

AMIGO

¡Ríete! *[Le hace cosquillas.]*

FRIEND

What's to think! Anyway, I'm going. Even though . . . I . . . *[Looks at his watch]* I'm late already. It's terrible, the same thing always. I have no time, and I regret it. I was supposed to go out with the ugliest woman, you hear? Ha, ha, ha, ha, so ugly, but adorable. A brunette of the sort you start to miss on a summer's afternoon, and I like her *[Throws a cushion in the air]* because she reminds me of a horse trainer.

YOUNG MAN

That's enough!

FRIEND

Yes, man, don't look so disgusted. A woman can be very ugly and a horse trainer beautiful, and vice versa, and . . . who knows? *[Fills a cocktail glass]*

YOUNG MAN

No one.

FRIEND

Would you mind telling me what is the matter with you?

YOUNG MAN

Nothing. You know how I am, don't you? It's my temperament.

FRIEND

I can't understand it. I don't understand, but I won't be solemn either. *[Laughs]* I'll greet you as they do in China. *[Rubs his nose against the YOUNG MAN's]*

YOUNG MAN

[Smiling] Stop it!

FRIEND

Laugh! *[Tickles him]*

JOVEN

[Riendo] Bárbaro. *[Luchan.]*

AMIGO

Una plancha.

JOVEN

Puedo contigo.

AMIGO

Te cogí. *[Lo coge con la cabeza entre las piernas y le da golpes.]*[62]

VIEJO

[Entrando gravemente] Con permiso... *[Los jóvenes quedan de pie]* Perdonen... *[Enérgicamente y mirando al JOVEN]* Se me olvidará el sombrero.

AMIGO

[Asombrado] ¿Cómo?

VIEJO

[Furioso] ¡Sí, señor! Se me olvidará el sombrero... *[Entre dientes]* Es decir, se me ha olvidado el sombrero.

AMIGO

¡Ahhh!

[Se oye un estrépito de cristales.]

JOVEN

[En alta voz] Juan, cierra las ventanas.

AMIGO

Un poco de tormenta. ¡Ojalá sea fuerte!

JOVEN

¡Pues no quiero enterarme! *[En alta voz]* Todo bien cerrado.

YOUNG MAN

[Laughing] Barbarian. *[They fight.]*

FRIEND

A tackle.

YOUNG MAN

Not me, you don't.

FRIEND

Got you. *[Catches his head between his legs and beats on him.]*

OLD MAN

[Entering solemnly] Pardon me .... *[The young men get to their feet.]* Excuse me .... *[Emphatically and looking at the YOUNG MAN]* I am going to forget my hat.

FRIEND

[Amazed] What?

OLD MAN

[Infuriated] Yes, sir! I am going to forget my hat .... *[Murmuring]* I mean to say, I have forgotten my hat.

FRIEND

Ohhhhhh!

[Sound of breaking glass.]

YOUNG MAN

[Out loud] Shut the windows, Juan!

FRIEND

A bit of a storm. A big one, I hope!

YOUNG MAN

Well, I don't want to know about it! *[Out loud]* All shut tight.

AMIGO

¡Los truenos tendrás que oirlos![63]

VIEJO

¡O no!

AMIGO

¡O sí!

JOVEN

No me importa lo que pase fuera. Esta casa es mía y aquí no entra nadie.

VIEJO

[Indignado al AMIGO] ¡Es una verdad sin refutación posible!

[Se oye un trueno lejano.]

AMIGO

[Apasionado] Entrará todo el mundo que quiera, no aquí, sino debajo de tu cama.[64]

[Trueno más cercano.]

JOVEN

[Gritando] Pero ahora, ¡ahora no!

VIEJO

¡Bravo!

AMIGO

¡Abre la ventana! Tengo calor.

VIEJO

¡Ya se abrirá!

JOVEN

¡Luego!

FRIEND

You'll have to hear the thunder!

OLD MAN

No he won't!

FRIEND

Yes he will!

YOUNG MAN

It doesn't matter what happens outside, but this house is mine, and no one gets in here.

OLD MAN

[Indignantly to the FRIEND] An irrefutable truth!

[Distant thunder sounds.]

FRIEND

[Passionately] Anyone who wants to can get in, not here, but under your bed.

[Closer thunder.]

YOUNG MAN

[Shouting] But not here, not now!

OLD MAN

Bravo!

FRIEND

Open the window! It's hot.

OLD MAN

It will be open soon enough!

YOUNG MAN

Later!

AMIGO

Pero, vamos a ver . . .[65]

[*Se oye otro trueno. La luz desciende y una luminosidad azulada de tormenta invade la escena. Los tres personajes se ocultarán detrás de un biombo negro bordado con estrellas.*[66] *Por la puerta de la izquierda aparece el NIÑO MUERTO con el GATO. El NIÑO viene vestido de blanco primera comunión, con una corona de rosas blancas en la cabeza. Sobre su rostro, pintado de cera, resaltan sus ojos y sus labios de lirio seco. Trae un cirio rizado en la mano y el gran lazo con flecos de oro. El GATO es azul con dos enormes manchas rojas de sangre en el pechito*[67] *gris y en la cabeza. Avanzan hacia el público. El NIÑO trae al GATO cogido de una pata.*]

GATO

Miau.

NIÑO

Chisssssss.

GATO

Miauuu.

NIÑO

Toma mi pañuelo blanco.
Toma mi corona blanca.
No llores más.

GATO

Me duelen las heridas
que los niños me hicieron en la espalda.[68]

NIÑO

También a mí me duele el corazón.

GATO

¿Por qué te duele, niño, di?

FRIEND

But, let's see . . . .

[More thunder. The light dims and the blue light of a storm pervades the scene. The three characters will conceal themselves behind a black screen embroidered with stars. From the door at left, the DEAD BOY and the CAT appear. The BOY is dressed in white, as though for his first communion, with a crown of white roses on his head. His face is waxen, and his eyes and his dry-lily lips are prominent against it. He carries an ornate candle in his hand, adorned with a great gold-fringed bow. The CAT is blue with two huge red bloodstains on its gray chest and on its head. They come forward towards the audience, the BOY leading the CAT by one paw.]

CAT

Meow.

BOY

Shhhhhhh.

CAT

Meoooow.

BOY

I'll give you my white handkerchief.
And I'll give you my white halo.
Don't cry anymore.

CAT

                 The children hit me
all over my poor back. It hurts me so.

BOY

And I have a terrible pain in my heart.

CAT

Oh why, boy, why?

NIÑO

                                        Porque no anda.
Ayer se me paró muy despacito,
ruiseñor de mi cama.
Mucho ruido, ¡si vieras . . . ! Me pusieron
con estas rosas frente a la ventana.[69]

GATO

¿Y qué sentías tú?

NIÑO

                                Pues yo sentía
surtidores y abejas por la sala.
Me ataron las dos manos, ¡muy mal hecho!
Los niños por los vidrios me miraban.
Y un hombre con martillo iba clavando
estrellas de papel sobre mi caja.[70]
No vinieron los ángeles. No, Gato.

GATO

¡No me digas más gato!

NIÑO

                                ¿No?

GATO

                                        Soy gata.

NIÑO

¿Eres gata?

GATO

[Mimosa]   Debiste conocerlo.

NIÑO

¿Por qué?

BOY

Because it doesn't go.
Yesterday it ran down and it stopped,
the nightingale of my pillow.
Such noise, if you'd seen it...! They laid me out
beside the window with this crown of rose.

CAT

And how did you feel?

BOY

Oh, how did I feel?
I felt bubbles and bees in the patio.
They tied my hands together...badly done!...
and the children looked in through the window.
There was a man with a hammer who drove
paper stars in my coffin in rows.
No angels appeared to me. No, cat, no.

CAT

Please don't say cat.

BOY

No?

CAT

I'm a lady!

BOY

Oh.

You're a lady?

CAT

[Fondly]   Well, you ought to have known.

BOY

How could I?

GATO

Por mi voz de plata.[71]

NIÑO

[Galante] ¿No te quieres sentar?

GATO

Sí. Tengo hambre.

NIÑO

Voy a ver si te encuentro alguna rata.

[Se pone a mirar debajo de las sillas . . . El GATO sentado en un taburete tiembla.]

No[72] la comas entera. Una patita,
porque estás muy enferma.

GATO

Diez pedradas
me tiraron los niños.

NIÑO

Pesan como las rosas
que oprimieron[73] anoche mi garganta.
¿Quieres una?

[Se arranca una rosa de la cabeza.]

GATO

[Alegre] Sí, quiero.

NIÑO

Con tus manchas de cera, rosa blanca,
ojo de luna rota me pareces
o gacela entre[74] vidrios desmayada.

[Se la pone.]

GATO

¿Tú qué hacías?

CAT

Of course, by my silvery tones.

BOY

[Gallant] Won't you be seated?

CAT

Yes, please. I'm hungry.

BOY

A rat is what you need. I'll find you one.

[He begins to look under the chairs. Seated on a stool, the CAT trembles.]

Don't swallow it whole now. Just one leg.
Because you're not feeling so well.

CAT

Ten stones

those children hit me with.

BOY

As heavy as the roses
that pressed all night long on my throat.
Would you like one?

[He plucks a rose from his head.]

CAT

[Brightly]   Oh yes, I would.

BOY

With your little spots of wax, white rose,
you look like the eye of a broken moon
or a fawn collapsed among the windows.

[He puts it on her.]

CAT

What were you doing?

NIÑO

Jugar. ¿Y tú?

GATO

¡Jugar!

Iba por el tejado, gata chata,
naricillas de hojadelata.
En la mañana
iba a coger[75] los peces por el agua
y al mediodía
bajo el rosal del muro me dormía.

NIÑO

¿Y por la noche?

GATO

[Enfático]

Me iba sola.

NIÑO

¿Sin nadie?[76]

GATO

Por el bosque.

NIÑO

[Con alegría]

Yo también iba, ¡ay!, gata chata, barata,
naricillas de hojadelata,
a comer zarzamoras y manzanas.[77]
Y después a la Iglesia con los niños
a jugar a la cabra.

GATO

¿Qué es la cabra?

NIÑO

Era mamar los clavos de la puerta.

BOY

Playing. You?

CAT

Playing.
I was walking on the roof. Button nose,
there she goes, she ain't telling what she knows.
In the morning glow,
I went out to catch fish, don't you know,
and at noon,
I slept by the wall where the rose tree grows.

BOY

And at night?

CAT

[Insistent]

I was alone.

BOY

By yourself?

CAT

In the woods.

BOY

[Brightly]

Ah! I was out too, button nose, tiny toes,
there she goes, she ain't telling what she knows,
out where apples and blackberries grow.
And then at the church with my friends
playing The Goat.

CAT

What is The Goat?

BOY

Sucking the nails on the door.

GATO

¿Y eran buenos?

NIÑO

No, gata,
como chupar monedas.[78]

[Trueno lejano]

¡Ay! ¡Espera! ¿No vienen? Tengo miedo.
¿Sabes? Me escapé de casa.

[Lloroso]

Yo no quiero que me entierren.
Agremanes[79] y vidrios adornan mi caja;
pero es mejor que me duerma
entre los juncos del agua.
Yo no quiero que me entierren. ¡Vamos pronto!

[Le tira de la pata.][80]

GATO

¿Y nos van a enterrar? ¿Cuándo?

NIÑO

Mañana.

En unos hoyos oscuros.[81]
Todos lloran, todos callan.
Pero se van. Yo lo ví.
Y luego ¿sabes? . . .

GATO

¿Qué pasa?

NIÑO

Vienen a comernos.

CAT

Did they taste good?

BOY

Oh lady, no,
like chewing on a bunch of coins.

[Distant thunder]

Oh wait! They aren't coming, are they? I'm afraid.
Do you know what? I ran away from home.

[Tearfully]

I don't want them to bury me.
My coffin is covered with glass and silk bows;
but I would rather go to sleep
by the water in the reeds. I don't
want to be buried. Let's get out of here!

[He pulls her by the paw.]

CAT

We're going to be buried? When?

BOY

Tomorrow.

In a couple of dark, dark holes.
Everybody's silent, or they moan.
Then they go. I've seen it happen.
And then, you know what?

CAT

What? I don't.

BOY

They come and they eat us.

GATO

¿Quién?

NIÑO

El lagarto y la lagarta
con sus hijos[82] pequeños que son muchos.

GATO

¿Y qué nos comen?

NIÑO

La cara
con los dedos *[bajando la voz]* y la cuca.

GATO

[Ofendida]

Yo no tengo cuca.

NIÑO

[Enérgico]   ¡Gata!:
te comerán las patas[83] y el bigote.

[Trueno lejanísimo]

Vámonos de casa en casa,
llegaremos donde pacen
los caballitos del agua.
No es el cielo. Es tierra dura,
con muchos grillos que cantan,
con hierbas que se menean,
con nubes que se levantan,
con hondas que lanzan piedras
y el viento como una espada.
¡Yo quiero ser niño! ¡Un niño!

[Se dirige a la puerta de la derecha.]

GATO

Está la puerta cerrada.
Vámonos por la escalera.

CAT

    Who does?

BOY

Mr. and Mrs. Lizard do,
with their countless little kids.

CAT

What parts will they eat?

BOY

                Our noses
and our fingers *[lowering his voice]* and our peepees.

CAT

[Offended] I haven't got a peepee.

BOY

[Forcefully]   No?
    Then they'll eat your paws and whiskers.

[Very distant thunder.]

    Come, let's get out of here. We'll go
from house to house until we reach
the place where the seahorses graze.
It isn't heaven. It's solid ground,
with the grass swaying to and fro,
and a lot of crickets chirping,
and slingshots for shooting stones,
and the wind just like a sword,
and the clouds all floating over.
I want to be a boy! A boy!

[He goes towards the door at right.]

CAT

Not that way. The door is closed.
Come on, let's try the stairs.

NIÑO

Por la escalera nos verán.

GATO

Aguarda.

NIÑO

¡Ya vienen para enterrarnos!

GATO

Vámonos por la ventana.

NIÑO

Nunca veremos la luz,
ni nubes[84] que se levantan,
ni los grillos en la hierba,
ni al viento[85] como una espada.

[Cruzando las manos]

¡Ay girasol!
¡Ay girasol de fuego!
¡Ay girasol!

GATO

¡Ay clavellina del sol!

NIÑO

Apagado va el cielo.[86]
Sólo mares y montes de carbón.
Y una paloma muerta por la arena
con las alas tronchadas y en el pico una flor.

[Canta]

"Y en la flor una oliva
y en la oliva un limón..."
¿Cómo sigue?... ¡No lo sé! ¿Cómo sigue?

GATO

¡Ay girasol!
¡Ay girasol de la mañanita!
¡Ay girasol!

BOY

They'd see us on the stairs.

CAT

Oh no.

BOY

Here they come now to bury us!

CAT

Come on, we can try the window.

BOY

We'll never see the light again,
or the clouds all floating over,
or the crickets in the tall grass,
or the wind like a sword.

[Crossing his hands]

Oh sunflower!
Sunflower of blood!
Oh sunflower!

CAT

Carnation of the sun!

BOY

The light has gone out of the sky.
Only mountains of coal and coal seas,
and a dove lying dead on the sand,
her wings snapped off and a flower in her beak.

[He sings.]

"And inside the flower an olive,
and inside the olive a lime . . . ."
How does it go? I don't know. How's it go?

CAT

Oh sunflower!
Sunflower of the dawn!
Oh sunflower!

NIÑO

¡Ay clavellina del sol!

[La luz es tenue. El NIÑO y el GATO, separados,[87] andan a tientas.]

GATO

No hay luz. ¿Dónde estás?

NIÑO

¡Calla!

GATO

¿Vendrán ya los lagartos, niño?

NIÑO

No.

GATO

¿Encontraste salida?

[El GATO se acerca a la puerta de la derecha y sale una mano que lo empuja hacia dentro.]

GATO

[Con angustia] ¡Niño! ¡Niño!

[Dentro]

¡Niño! ¡Niño![88]

[El NIÑO avanza con terror, deteniéndose a cada paso.]

NIÑO

[En voz baja]

Se hundió.
Lo ha cogido una mano.
Debe ser la de Dios.
¡No me entierres! Espera unos minutos...
¡Mientras deshojo esta flor!

[Se arranca una flor de la cabeza y la deshoja.]

Yo iré solo, muy despacio,

BOY

Carnation of the sun!

[The light dims. Separated, the BOY and the CAT grope about.]

CAT

I can't see. Where are you?

BOY

Quiet!

CAT

Now do the lizards come, boy?

BOY

No.

CAT

Did you find the way out?

[The CAT goes to the door at right. Enter a hand that pulls her off.]

CAT

[In anguish] Boy! Oh!

[Off]

Boy! Boy!

[The boy goes on in terror, stopping at every step.]

BOY

[In a soft voice]
She's disappeared.
A hand has taken her below.
It must have been the hand of God.
Don't bury me! Wait a minute or so . . .
while I pull this flower's petals off!

[He plucks a flower from his head and pulls the petals off.]
I'll go willingly, but slow;

después me dejarás mirar al sol . . .
Muy poco, con un rayo me contento.

[Deshojando]

Sí, no, sí, no, sí.

VOZ

NO.[89]

[La mano asoma y entra al NIÑO que se desmaya. La luz al desaparecer el NIÑO vuelve a su tono primero. Por detrás del biombo vuelven a salir rápidamente los tres personajes. Dan muestras de calor y de agitación viva. El JOVEN lleva un abanico azul, el VIEJO un abanico negro y el AMIGO un abanico rojo agresivo. Se abanican.]

VIEJO

Pues todavía *será*[90] más.

JOVEN

Sí. Después.

AMIGO

Ya ha sido bastante. Creo que no te puedes escapar de la tormenta.[91]

VOZ

[Fuera] ¡Mi hijo! ¡Mi hijo!

JOVEN

¡Señor, qué tarde! Juan: ¿quién grita así?

CRIADO

[Entrando[92] siempre en tono suave y andando sobre las puntas de los pies.] El niño[93] de la portera murió y ahora lo llevan a enterrar. Su madre llora.

AMIGO

¡Como es natural!

VIEJO[94]

Sí,sí; pero lo pasado, pasado.

you'll let me see the sun, I hope . . . .
Just a little, one ray will do.

[Pulling petals off]

Yes, no, yes, no, yes.

VOICE

NO.

[The hand comes in and carries off the BOY, who faints. As the BOY disappears, the light returns to its previous tone. The three characters reappear quickly from behind the screen. They seem hot and quite agitated. The YOUNG MAN carries a blue fan, the OLD MAN a black fan and the FRIEND an aggressive red fan. They fan themselves.]

OLD MAN

Well, there *will* be more later.

YOUNG MAN

Yes. Later.

FRIEND

It's open quite enough already. I believe that you cannot escape the storm.

VOICE

[Off] My son! My son!

YOUNG MAN

Lord, what an afternoon! Who's that screaming, Juan?

SERVANT

[Entering with a smooth voice and as always on tiptoe] The concierge's boy has died, and they are now on their way to bury him. His mother is crying.

FRIEND

Quite naturally!

OLD MAN

Yes, yes; but what's past is past.

AMIGO

Pero si ¡está pasando! *[Discuten]*

[El CRIADO cruza la escena y va a salir por la puerta de la izquierda.]

CRIADO

Señor: ¿Tendría[95] la bondad de dejarme la llave de su dormitorio?

JOVEN

¿Para qué?

CRIADO

Los niños[96] arrojaron un gato que habían matado sobre el tejadillo del jardín y hay necesidad de quitarlo.

JOVEN

[Con fastidio] Toma. *[Al VIEJO]* ¡No podrá usted con él![97]

VIEJO

Ni me interesa.

AMIGO

No es verdad. Sí le interesa. Al que no le interesa es a mí, que sé positivamente que la nieve es fría y que el fuego quema.

VIEJO

[Irónico] ¡Según!

AMIGO

[Al JOVEN] Te está engañando.

[El VIEJO mira enérgicamente al AMIGO, estrujando su sombrero.]

JOVEN

[Con fuerza] No influye lo más mínimo en mi carácter.[98] Soy yo. Pero tú no puedes comprender que se espere a una mujer cinco años, colmado y quemado por el amor que crece cada día.

FRIEND

But it's passing right now! *[They argue]*

[The SERVANT crosses the stage and is about to exit by the door at left.]

SERVANT

Sir, would you be so kind as to let me have the key to your bedroom?

YOUNG MAN

What for?

SERVANT

The children have thrown a cat they killed onto the garden awning, and it will be necessary to remove it.

YOUNG MAN

[Testily] Here. *[To the OLD MAN]* You won't convince him!

OLD MAN

Not that I care to.

FRIEND

That isn't true. He does care to. The one who doesn't care is me, because I've never doubted for a moment that snow is cold and fire burns.

OLD MAN

[Ironical] That depends!

FRIEND

[To the YOUNG MAN] He's got you fooled.

[The OLD MAN looks emphatically at the FRIEND, while squeezing on his hat.]

YOUNG MAN

[Forcefully] He hasn't the least influence on my character. I'm me. But you just can't understand how one could wait five years for a woman, filled and seared by a love that grows stronger every day.

AMIGO

¡No hay necesidad de esperar!

JOVEN

¿Crees tú que yo puedo vencer las cosas materiales, los obstáculos que surgen y se aumentarán en el camino sin causar dolor a los demás?[99]

AMIGO

¡Primero eres tú que los demás!

JOVEN

Esperando; el nudo se deshace y la fruta madura.

AMIGO

Yo prefiero comerla verde, o mejor todavía, me gusta cortar su flor para ponerla en mi solapa.[100]

VIEJO

¡No es verdad!

AMIGO

¡Usted es demasiado viejo para saberlo!

VIEJO

[Severamente] Yo he luchado toda mi vida por encender una luz en los sitios más oscuros. Y cuando la gente ha ido a retorcer el cuello de la paloma, yo he sujetado la mano y la he ayudado a volar.

AMIGO

¡Y, naturalmente, el cazador[101] se ha muerto de hambre!

JOVEN

¡Bendita sea el hambre!

[Aparece por la puerta de la izquierda el AMIGO SEGUNDO. Viene vestido de blanco, con un impecable traje de lana y lleva guantes y zapatos del mismo color. De no ser posible que este papel lo haga un actor muy joven, lo hará una muchacha. El traje ha

FRIEND

You don't need to wait!

YOUNG MAN

You think I can overcome solid matter, all the obstacles that arise and grow more numerous along the way without hurting anybody?

FRIEND

You come first, before anybody else!

YOUNG MAN

When one waits, the knot untangles and the fruit gets ripe.

FRIEND

I prefer to eat it green, or better still, I like to snip its blossom to wear on my lapel.

OLD MAN

That's not true!

FRIEND

You're too old to understand!

OLD MAN

[Sternly] All my life, I have fought to light a lamp in the darkest places. And when somebody has tried to break the neck of a dove, I've stayed their hand and helped her fly away.

FRIEND

And naturally, the hunter died of hunger!

OLD MAN

Blessed be hunger!

[Through the door at left, the SECOND FRIEND appears. He is dressed in white, in an impeccable wool suit, with gloves and shoes of the same color. If it is not possible for a very young actor to take this part, it should be taken by a girl. The suit should be of a very

de ser de un corte exageradísimo, llevará enormes botones azules y el chaleco y la corbata serán de rizados encajes.]

AMIGO 2

Bendita sea, cuando hay pan tostado, aceite y sueño después. Mucho sueño. Que no se acabe nunca. Te he oído.

JOVEN

[Con asombro] ¿Por dónde has entrado?

AMIGO 2

Por cualquier sitio. Por la ventana. Me ayudaron dos niños amigos míos. Los conocí cuando yo era muy pequeño y me han empujado por los pies. Va a caer un aguacero . . . , pero aguacero bonito el que cayó el año pasado. Había tan poca luz que se me pusieron las manos amarillas. *[Al VIEJO]* ¿Lo recuerda usted?[102]

VIEJO

[Agrio] No recuerdo nada.

AMIGO 2

[Al AMIGO 1] ¿Y tú?

AMIGO 1

[Serio] ¡Tampoco!

AMIGO 2

Yo era muy pequeño, pero lo recuerdo con todo detalle.[103]

AMIGO 1

Mira . . .

AMIGO 2

Por eso no quiero ver éste. La lluvia es hermosa. En el colegio entraba por los patios y estrellaba por las paredes a unas mujeres desnudas, muy pequeñas, que lleva dentro. ¿No las habéis visto? Cuando yo tenía cinco años . . . , no, cuando yo tenía dos . . . , ¡miento!, uno, un año tan sólo, ¡es hermoso!, ¿verdad?, un año.

exaggerated cut; it has enormous blue buttons, and the vest and tie are of ruffled lace.]

SECOND FRIEND

Blessed indeed, so long as there's toast and olive oil and then to dreamland. For a long dream. Never ending. I overheard you.

YOUNG MAN

[Amazed] How did you get in here?

SECOND FRIEND

Somehow, I don't know. Through the window. Two children helped me, my good friends. I met them when I was very little. They boosted me in by my feet. It's really going to pour..., but how lovely the way it poured last year. There was so little light that my hands turned yellow. *[To the OLD MAN]* Do you remember?

OLD MAN

[Sourly] I remember nothing.

SECOND FRIEND

[To the FIRST FRIEND] And you?

FIRST FRIEND

[Solemn] Me neither.

SECOND FRIEND

I was so little, but I remember every detail.

FIRST FRIEND

Look ....

SECOND FRIEND

That's why I don't want to see it this time. Rain is beautiful. At school it would get into the patios and cause the little naked women, so tiny, who live in the raindrops, to appear against the walls. Have you never seen them? When I was five ... no, when I was two.... It's a lie! When I was one, just one, it's beautiful!

Cogí una de estas mujercillas de la lluvia y la tuve dos días en una pecera.

AMIGO 1

[Con sorna] ¿Y creció?

AMIGO 2

¡No! Se hizo cada vez más pequeña, más niña, como debe ser, como es lo justo, hasta que no quedó de ella más que una gota de agua. Y cantaba una canción...

> Yo vuelvo por mis alas
> ¡dejadme volver!
> ¡Quiero morirme siendo
> amanecer!
> ¡Quiero morirme siendo
> ayer!
> Yo vuelvo por mis alas
> ¡dejadme retornar!
> ¡Quiero morirme siendo
> manantial!
> ¡Quiero morirme fuera
> de la mar![104]

Que es exáctamente[105] lo que yo canto a todas horas.

VIEJO

[Irritado, al JOVEN] Está completamente loco.

AMIGO 2

[Que lo ha oído] ¿Loco?, porque no quiero estar lleno de arrugas y dolores como usted. Porque quiero vivir lo mío y me lo quitan. Yo no lo conozco a usted. Yo no quiero ver gente como usted.

AMIGO 1

[Bebiendo] Todo eso no es más que miedo a la muerte.

AMIGO 2

No. Ahora; antes de entrar aquí, ví a un niño que llevaban a enterrar con las primeras gotas de la lluvia. Así quiero que me entierren a

Truly. One year old. I caught one of these little rain women and kept her for two days in a fishbowl.

FIRST FRIEND

[Sarcastically] And did she grow?

SECOND FRIEND

No! She just got littler, more like a girl, just as she should have, as was right, until there was nothing left of her but a drop of water. And she sang a song . . . .

> I'll go back for my wings,
> I must be away!
> I want to die at
> the break of day!
> I want to die just
> yesterday!

> I'll go back for my wings,
> Away I must be!
> I want to die as a drop
> in a stream!
> I want to die outside
> the sea!

Which is exactly what I always sing.

OLD MAN

[Irritated, to YOUNG MAN] He's completely out of his mind.

SECOND FRIEND

[Who has heard him] Out of my mind? Because I don't want to be full of aches and wrinkles like yourself. Because I want to live what's mine, and it's taken from me. I don't know you. I don't want to see you or anybody like you.

FIRST FRIEND

[Drinking] All that's nothing but the fear of death.

SECOND FRIEND

No. Just now, as I was coming in, I saw a boy they were about to bury with the first drops of rain. That's how I'd like to be buried.

mí. En una caja así de pequeña. Y ustedes se van a luchar en[106] la borrasca. Pero mi rostro es mío y me lo están robando. Yo era tierno y cantaba y ahora hay un hombre, un señor, *[al VIEJO]* como usted que anda por dentro de mí, con dos o tres caretas preparadas. *[Saca un espejo y se mira]* Pero todavía no; todavía me veo subido en los cerezos... con aquel traje gris... Un traje gris que tenía unas anclas de plata... ¡Dios mío! *[Se cubre la cara con las manos.]*

VIEJO

Los trajes se rompen, las anclas se oxidan y vamos adelante.

AMIGO 2

¡Oh, por favor, no hable así!

VIEJO

[Entusiasmado] Se hunden las casas.

AMIGO 1

[Enérgico y en actitud de defensa] Las casas no se hunden.

VIEJO

[Impertérrito] Se apagan los ojos y una hoz muy afilada siega los juncos de las orillas.

AMIGO 2

[Sereno][107] ¡Claro! ¡Todo eso pasa más adelante!

VIEJO

[Enérgico] Al contrario. Eso *ha pasado*[108] ya.

AMIGO 2

Atrás se queda todo quieto. ¿Cómo es posible que no lo sepa usted? No hay más que ir despertando suavemente las cosas.[109] En cambio, dentro de cuatro o cinco años existe un pozo en el que caeremos todos.

In a coffin that little. And you all can fight in the storm. But my face belongs to me, and it's being stolen from me. I was soft and I used to sing, and now there's a man, a gentleman *[To the OLD MAN]* like you walking around inside of me with two or three masks all ready. *[Takes out a mirror and looks at himself]* But not quite yet; I can still see myself climbing in the cherry trees . . . in that gray sailor suit . . . a gray suit with silver anchors . . . . My God! *[Covers his face with his hands]*

OLD MAN

Clothes wear out, anchors rust, and we go forward.

SECOND FRIEND

Oh, please don't say that!

OLD MAN

[Enthusiastic] Houses crumble.

FIRST FRIEND

[Emphatic and on the defensive] Houses do not crumble.

OLD MAN

[Undaunted] The eyes grow dim and a razor-sharp sickle reaps the reeds along the riverbanks.

SECOND FRIEND

[Serene] Of course! Much more time will pass before any of this happens!

OLD MAN

[Emphatic] On the contrary. It *has passed* already.

SECOND FRIEND

Behind us, everything is still. Didn't you know that? We just go on, gently waking things up. Unfortunately, in four or five years, we'll all fall into the well that's waiting for us.

VIEJO

[Furioso] ¡Silencio!

JOVEN

[Temblando, al VIEJO] ¿Lo ha oido usted?

VIEJO

Demasiado. *[Sale rápidamente por la puerta de la derecha.]*

JOVEN

[Detrás] ¿Dónde va usted? ¿Por qué se marcha así? ¡Espere!
[Sale detrás.]

AMIGO 2

[Encogiéndose de hombros] Bueno. Viejo tenía que ser. Usted, en cambio, no ha protestado.

AMIGO 1

[Que ha estado bebiendo sin parar] No.

AMIGO 2

Usted, con beber tiene bastante.

AMIGO 1

[Serio y cara borracha][110] Yo hago lo que me gusta, ¡lo que me parece
bien! No le he pedido su parecer.

AMIGO 2

[Con miedo] Si, si...[111] Yo no le digo nada...

[Se sienta en un sillón con las piernas encogidas.]

> *[El AMIGO 1 se bebe rápidamente dos copas, apuradas hasta lo
> último*[112] *y dándose un golpe en la frente, como si recordara algo,
> sale rápidamente, en medio de una alegrísima sonrisa,*[113] *por la
> puerta de la izquierda. El AMIGO 2 inclina la cabeza en el sillón.
> Aparece el CRIADO por la derecha, siempre delicado, sobre las
> puntas de los pies. Empieza a llover.]*

OLD MAN

[Infuriated] Silence!

YOUNG MAN

[Trembling, to the OLD MAN] You hear what he says?

OLD MAN

I've heard enough. *[Exits rapidly through the door at right]*

YOUNG MAN

[Following] Where are you going? Why are you leaving like this? Wait! *[Exits following]*

SECOND FRIEND

[Shrugging] Well. It's obvious he's an old man. You, on the other hand, didn't protest.

FIRST FRIEND

[Who has been drinking without pause] No.

SECOND FRIEND

For you, it's enough just to drink.

FIRST FRIEND

[Solemn and pasty-faced] I do whatever I like, whatever seems best to me! I didn't ask your opinion.

SECOND FRIEND

[Afraid] But, but . . . I'm not trying to tell you . . . .

[He sits down in an armchair with his legs drawn up.]

> *[The FIRST FRIEND quickly swallows two drinks more, draining them dry, and striking his forehead as though he'd just remembered something, he exits quickly, with a broad and happy smile, through the door at left. The SECOND FRIEND leans his head against the chair. The SERVANT appears from right, always delicate, on tiptoe. It begins to rain.]*

AMIGO 2

El aguacero. *[Se mira las manos]* Pero qué luz más fea. *[Queda dormido.]*

JOVEN

[Entrando] Mañana volverá. Lo necesito.

[Se sienta.]

> *[Aparece la MECANOGRAFA. Lleva una maleta. Cruza la escena y, en medio de ella, se[114] vuelve rápidamente.]*

MECANOGRAFA

¿Me habías llamado?

JOVEN

[Cerrando los ojos] No.[115]

> *[La MECANOGRAFA sale mirando con ansia y esperando la llamada.]*

MECANOGRAFA

[En la puerta] ¿Me necesitas?

JOVEN

[Cerrando los ojos] No. No te necesito.

> *[Sale la MECANOGRAFA.]*

AMIGO 2

[Entre sueños]

> Yo vuelvo por mis alas
> ¡dejadme volver!
> ¡Quiero morirme siendo
> ayer!
> ¡Quiero morirme siendo
> amanecer!

[Empieza a llover]

JOVEN

Es demasiado tarde. Juan, enciende las luces. ¿Qué hora es?

SECOND FRIEND

It's pouring. *[Looks at his hands]* What nasty light. *[Falls asleep]*

YOUNG MAN

[Entering] He'll be back tomorrow. I need him.

[He sits down.]

> *[The TYPIST appears. She has a suitcase. She crosses the stage, and in the middle, she turns quickly around.]*

TYPIST

You called me?

YOUNG MAN

[Closing his eyes] No.

> *[The TYPIST exits looking around anxiously and waiting to be called.]*

TYPIST

[At the door] You need me?

YOUNG MAN

[Closing his eyes] No. I don't need you.

> *[The TYPIST exits.]*

SECOND FRIEND

[In dream]

> I'll go back for my wings,
> I must be away!
> I want to die just
> yesterday!
> I want to die at
> the break of day!

> *[It starts to rain.]*

YOUNG MAN

It's getting late. Juan, turn on the lights. What time is it?

JUAN

[Con intención] Las seis en punto, señor.

JOVEN

Está bien.

AMIGO 2

[Entre sueños)

Yo vuelvo por mis alas
¡dejadme retornar![116]
¡Quiero morirme siendo
manantial!
¡Quiero morirme fuera
de la mar!

[El JOVEN golpea suavemente la mesa con los dedos.]

Telón lento

Acto Segundo

Alcoba estilo 1900. Muebles extraños. Grandes cortinajes llenos de
pliegues y borlas. Por las paredes, nubes y ángeles pintados. En el
centro, una cama llena de colgaduras y plumajes. A la izquierda,
un tocador sostenido por ángeles con ramos de luces eléctricas en
las manos. Los balcones están abiertos y por ellos entra la luna. Se
oye un cláxon de automóvil que toca con furia. La NOVIA salta
de la cama con espléndida bata llena de encajes y enormes lazos
color de rosa. Lleva una larga cola y todo el cabello hecho bucles.[1]

NOVIA

[Asomándose al balcón] Sube.*[Se oye el cláxon]* Es preciso. Llegará mi
novio, el viejo, el lírico y necesito apoyarme en tí.

*[El JUGADOR DE RUGBY[2] entra por el balcón. Viene vestido
con las rodilleras, el casco y una bolsa llena de cigarros puros que
enciende y aplasta sin cesar.]*

NOVIA

Entra. Hace dos días que no te veo.*[Se abrazan]*

SERVANT

[Willfully] Six on the dot, sir.

YOUNG MAN

That's fine.

SECOND FRIEND

[In dream]

> I'll go back for my wings,
> Away I must be!
> I want to die as a drop
> in a stream.
> I want to die outside
> the sea.

[The YOUNG MAN gently drums on the table with his fingers.]

Slow curtain

Act Two

Bedroom in turn-of-the-century style. Strange furniture. Great curtains full of pleats and tassels. Clouds and angels painted on the walls. At center, a bed full of hangings and plumes. At left, a dressing table held up by angels with branches of electric lights in their hands. The balconies are wide open, and the moonlight comes in through them. The sound of a car horn, furiously honking, is heard. The FIANCÉE jumps from her bed, wearing a splendid dressing gown, covered with lace and great rose-colored bows. She has a long train, and her hair is all in ringlets.

FIANCÉE

[Going to the balcony] Come on up. *[The horn sounds.]* You've got to. My fiancé is on his way—the old one, the poet—and I need to lean on you.

> *[The FOOTBALL PLAYER enters from the balcony. He is wearing his kneepads and his helmet, and he has a pocket full of cigars, which he lights and extinguishes, one after another.]*

FIANCÉE

Come here. It's two days since I've seen you. *[They embrace.]*

[El JUGADOR DE RUGBY no habla, sólo fuma y aplasta con el pie el cigarro,[3] da muestras de una gran vitalidad y abraza con ímpetu a la NOVIA.]

NOVIA

Hoy me has besado de una manera distinta. Siempre cambias, amor mío. Ayer no te ví, ¿sabes? Pero estuve viendo al caballo. Era hermoso: blanco y los cascos dorados[4] entre el heno de los pesebres.*[Se sientan en un sofá que hay al pie de la cama.]* Pero tú eres más hermoso: porque eres como un dragón. *[La abraza][5]* Creo que me vas a quebrar entre tus brazos, porque soy débil, porque soy pequeña, porque soy como la escarcha, porque soy como una diminuta guitarra quemada por el sol, y no me quiebras.[6]

[El JUGADOR DE RUGBY le echa el humo en la cara.]

NOVIA

[Pasándole las manos por el cuerpo][7] Detrás de toda esta sombra hay como una trabazón de puentes de plata para estrecharme a mí y para defenderme a mí que soy pequeñita como un botón, pequeñita como una abeja que entrara de pronto[8] en el salón del trono. ¿Verdad? ¿Verdad que sí?[9]

NOVIA

Me iré contigo.*[Apoya la cabeza en el pecho del JUGADOR]* Dragón, ¡dragón mío! ¿Cuántos corazones tienes? Hay en tu pecho como un torrente donde yo me voy a ahogar. Me voy a ahogar... *[lo mira]* y luego tú saldrás corriendo *[llora]* y me dejarás muerta por las orillas.

[El JUGADOR se lleva otro puro a la boca[10] y la NOVIA se lo enciende.]

¡Oh! *[Lo besa]* ¡Qué ascua blanca! ¡Qué fuego de marfil derraman tus dientes! Mi otro novio[11] tenía los dientes helados; me besaba y sus labios se le cubrían de pequeñas hojas marchitas: eran unos labios secos.[12] Yo me corté las trenzas porque le gustaban mucho, como ahora voy descalza porque te gusta a tí. ¿Verdad? ¿Verdad que sí? *[El JUGADOR la besa][13]* Y luego lo... Es preciso que nos vayamos.[14] Mi novio vendrá.

[The FOOTBALL PLAYER says nothing, just smokes and crushes the butts with a foot. He shows great vitality, embracing the FIANCÉE with energy.]

FIANCÉE

Your kiss is different today. You're always changing, my love. I didn't see you yesterday, you know, but I looked at your horse. He's so beautiful: white with hooves of gold in the manger hay. *[They sit on a sofa at the end of the bed.]* But not as beautiful as you are: because you are a dragon. *[He embraces her.]* I believe you could break me in two with your arms, as weak as I am, as small as I am, just like the frost, just like a tiny guitar burned in the sun, and you don't break me.

[The FOOTBALL PLAYER blows smoke in her face.]

FIANCÉE

[Running her hands over his body] There's a great silver bridge behind all this shadow, to span me and defend me, your little button, your little bee that suddenly got into the throne room. Isn't that true? Isn't it?

FIANCÉE

I'll come with you. *[Rests her head on the FOOTBALL PLAYER's chest]* Dragon, my dragon! How many hearts are in there? I'm drowning in the raging river in your chest. I'm drowning... *[Looks at him]* and then you'll run off *[Cries]* and leave me dead on the banks.

[The FOOTBALL PLAYER puts another cigar in his mouth, and the FIANCÉE lights it for him.]

Ah! *[Kisses him]* White hot embers, ivory fire runs from your teeth! My other fiancé's teeth were cold; he'd kiss me and little withered leaves would cover his lips; what dry lips they were. I cut my braids because they pleased him, the same as I go barefoot because you like me that way. Isn't that true? Isn't it? *[The FOOTBALL PLAYER kisses her.]* And then... I'm going to come with you. My fiancé is on his way.

VOZ

[En la puerta] ¡Señorita!

NOVIA

Vete.[15] *[Lo besa]*

VOZ

¡Señorita!

NOVIA

[Separándose del JUGADOR y adoptando una actitud distraída] ¡Ya voy![En voz baja]* ¡Adiós!

> *[El JUGADOR vuelve desde el balcón y le da un beso levantándola[16] en los brazos.]*

VOZ

¡Abra![17]

NOVIA

[Fingiendo la voz] ¡Qué poca paciencia!

> *[El JUGADOR sale silbando por el balcón.]*

CRIADA

[Entrando] ¡Ay señorita!

NOVIA

¿Qué señorita?

CRIADA

¡Señorita!

NOVIA

¿Qué?

> *[Enciende la luz del techo. Una luz más azulada que la que entra por los balcones.]*

VOICE

[At the door] Miss!

FIANCÉE

Coming. *[Kisses him]*

VOICE

Miss!

FIANCÉE

[Separating herself from the FOOTBALL PLAYER and affecting a distracted air] I'm coming! *[In a soft voice]* Goodbye!

> *[The FOOTBALL PLAYER comes back from the balcony and gives her a kiss, lifting her in his arms.]*

VOICE

Open up!

FIANCÉE

[In an affected voice] Have a little patience!

> *[The FOOTBALL PLAYER exits, whistling, by the balcony.]*

MAID

[Entering] Oh, miss!

FIANCÉE

What miss?

MAID

Miss!

FIANCÉE

What?

> *[The ceiling light goes up. More bluish than the light that comes in through the balconies.]*

CRIADA

¡Su novio ha llegado!

NOVIA

Bueno. ¿Por qué te pones así?

CRIADA

[Llorosa] Por nada.

NOVIA

¿Dónde está?

CRIADA

Abajo.

NOVIA

¿Con quién?

CRIADA

Con su padre.

NOVIA

¿Nadie más?

CRIADA

Y un señor con lentes de oro. Discutían mucho.[18]

NOVIA

Voy a vestirme. *[Se sienta delante del tocador y se arregla, ayudada de la CRIADA]*

CRIADA

[Llorosa] ¡Ay señorita!

NOVIA

[Irritada] ¿Qué señorita?

MAID

Your fiancé's here!

FIANCÉE

Fine. What's the trouble?

MAID

[Tearfully] Nothing.

FIANCÉE

Where is he?

MAID

Downstairs.

FIANCÉE

By himself?

MAID

With your father.

FIANCÉE

Nobody else?

MAID

And a gentleman in gold spectacles. They were having a big argument.

FIANCÉE

I'm going to get dressed. *[Sits at the dressing table and gets herself ready, assisted by the MAID]*

MAID

[Tearfully] Oh miss!

FIANCÉE

[Irritated] What miss?!

CRIADA

¡Señorita!

NOVIA

[Agria] ¡Qué![19]

CRIADA

Es muy guapo su novio.

NOVIA

Cásate con él.

CRIADA

Viene muy contento.

NOVIA

[Irónica][20] ¿Sí?

CRIADA

Traía un ramo de flores.[21]

NOVIA

Ya sabes que no me gustan las flores. Tira ésas por el balcón.[22]

CRIADA

¡Son tan hermosas! . . . Están recién cortadas.

NOVIA

[Autoritaria] ¡Tíralas!

> *[La CRIADA arroja unas flores, que estaban sobre un jarro, por el balcón.]*[23]

CRIADA

¡Ay señorita!

NOVIA

[Furiosa] ¿Qué señorita?

MAID

Miss!

FIANCÉE

[Sourly] What!

MAID

Your fiancé is so handsome.

FIANCÉE

Marry him yourself.

MAID

He's so happy.

FIANCÉE

[Ironical] Is he?

MAID

He brought you flowers.

FIANCÉE

You know I don't like flowers. Throw those out, off the balcony.

MAID

But they're beautiful . . . ! They're fresh cut.

FIANCÉE

[Peremptorily] Throw them out!

> *[The MAID discards some flowers, which were in a vase, off the balcony.]*

MAID

Oh miss!

FIANCÉE

[Infuriated] What miss?

CRIADA

¡Señorita!

NOVIA

¡Quéeee!

CRIADA

¡Piense bien en lo que hace![24] Recapacite. El mundo es grande. Pero las personas somos pequeñas.

NOVIA

¿Qué sabes tú?

CRIADA

Sí, sí lo sé. Mi padre estuvo en el Brasil dos veces . . . Y era tan chico que cabía en una maleta. Las cosas se olvidan. Y lo malo queda.

NOVIA

¡Te he dicho que te calles!

CRIADA

¡Ay señorita!

NOVIA

[Enérgica] ¡Mi ropa!

CRIADA

¡Qué va usted a hacer!

NOVIA

¡Lo que puedo!

CRIADA

¡Un hombre tan bueno! Con tanta ilusión. ¡Tánto tiempo esperándola! ¡Cinco años! ¡Cinco años![25]

[Le da los trajes.]

MAID

Miss!

FIANCÉE

Whaaaaat!

MAID

Consider what you're doing! Think of it. The world is large. But people like us are little.

FIANCÉE

What do you know?

MAID

Oh yes, I do know. My father was twice in Brazil . . . and he was so small he fit into a suitcase. Things are forgotten, but the bad remains.

FIANCÉE

I told you to keep quiet!

MAID

Oh miss!

FIANCÉE

[Emphatically] My clothes!

MAID

What are you going to do?

FIANCÉE

What I can!

MAID

Such a good man! With such hopes! Waiting so long! Five years! Five years!

[She gives her the dresses.]

NOVIA

¿Te dió la mano?

CRIADA

[Con alegría] Sí; me dió la mano.

NOVIA

¿Y cómo te dió la mano?

CRIADA

Muy delicadamente, casi sin apretar.

NOVIA

¿Lo ves? No te apretó.

CRIADA

Tuve un novio soldado que me clavaba los anillos y me hacía sangre. ¡Por eso lo despedí!

NOVIA

[Con sorna] ¿Sí?[26]

CRIADA

¡Ay señorita!

NOVIA

[Irritada][27] ¿Qué traje me pongo?

CRIADA

En el rojo[28] está preciosa.

NOVIA

No quiero estar guapa.

CRIADA

El verde.

FIANCÉE

Did he shake your hand?

MAID

[Happily] Yes; he shook my hand.

FIANCÉE

And how did he shake your hand?

MAID

Very gently, almost without squeezing.

FIANCÉE

You see? He didn't squeeze you.

MAID

I had a fiancé once who was a soldier. He crushed my rings against my fingers until they bled. That was why I left him!

FIANCÉE

[Sarcastically] Is that so?

MAID

Oh miss!

FIANCÉE

[Irritated] What dress shall I wear?

MAID

You look lovely in the red.

FIANCÉE

I don't want to look pretty.

MAID

The green.

NOVIA

[Suave][29] No.

CRIADA

El naranja.

NOVIA

[Fuerte] No.

CRIADA

El de tules.

NOVIA

[Más fuerte] No.

CRIADA

El traje hojas de Otoño.

NOVIA

[Irritada y fuerte] ¡He dicho que no! Quiero un hábito color tierra[30] para ese hombre; un hábito de roca pelada, con un cordón de esparto a la cintura.

[Se oye el cláxon. La NOVIA entorna los ojos y, cambiando la expresión, sigue hablando]

Pero con una corona de jazmines en el cuello y toda mi carne apretada por un velo mojado por el mar.*[Se dirige al balcón.]*

CRIADA

¡Que no se entere su novio!

NOVIA

Se ha de enterar.*[Eligiendo un traje de hábito sencillo]* Este. *[Se lo pone.]*

CRIADA

¡Está equivocada!

FIANCÉE

[Gently] No.

MAID

The orange?

FIANCÉE

[Forcefully] No.

MAID

The tulle.

FIANCÉE

[More forcefully] No.

MAID

The autumn leaves print.

FIANCÉE

[Forcefully and irritated] I said no! I want an earth-colored habit for that man, a habit of bare rock with a belt of hemp around the waist.

[The horn honks. The FIANCÉE half-closes her eyes and, with a changed expression, continues.]

But with a jasmine collar at my neck and my whole body wrapped tight in a veil wet by the sea. *[Goes to the balcony]*

MAID

Don't let your fiancé see!

FIANCÉE

Sooner or later, he's got to. *[Choosing a simple sack dress]* This one. *[Puts it on]*

MAID

You're wrong!

NOVIA

¿Por qué?

CRIADA

Su novio busca[31] otra cosa. En mi pueblo había un muchacho que subía a la torre de la iglesia para mirar más de cerca la luna, y su novia lo despidió.

NOVIA

¡Hizo bien!

CRIADA

Decía que veía en la luna el retrato de su novia.

NOVIA

[Enérgica] ¿Y a tí te parece bien?

> *[Se termina de arreglar en el tocador y enciende las luces de los ángeles.]*[32]

CRIADA

Sí, me parece bien. El muchacho la quería mucho.[33] Cuando yo me disgusté con el botones . . .

NOVIA

¿Ya te has disgustado ya con el botones? ¡Tan guapo! . . . ¡tan guapo! . . . ¡tan guapo! . . .

CRIADA

Naturalmente. Le regalé un pañuelo bordado por mí, que decía: "¡Amor! ¡Amor! ¡Amor!" Y se le perdió.[34]

NOVIA

Vete.

CRIADA

¿Cierro los balcones?

FIANCÉE

Why?

MAID

Your fiancé is looking for something else. There was a young man in my town who would climb up into the church tower to look more closely at the moon, and his fiancée left him.

FIANCÉE

She was right to!

MAID

He said he could see his fiancée's face in the moon.

FIANCÉE

[Emphatically] And you think that was right?

[She turns on the angel lamps to finish getting herself ready at the dressing table.]

MAID

Yes, I thought it was right. The young man loved her a lot. When I broke up with the bellboy . . . .

FIANCÉE

You broke up with the bellboy? So handsome . . . , so handsome . . . , so handsome . . . !

MAID

Naturally. I had given him a handkerchief that I'd embroidered myself, with the words, "Love!, Love!, Love!" He lost it.

FIANCÉE

Leave me.

MAID

Shall I close up the balconies?

NOVIA

No.

CRIADA

El aire le va a quemar el cutis.

NOVIA

Eso me gusta. Quiero ponerme negra. Más negra que un muchacho, y si me caigo no hacerme sangre y si agarro una zarzamora no herirme. Están todos andando por el alambre con los ojos cerrados. Y yo quiero tener plomo en los pies. Anoche soñaba que todos los niños pequeños crecen por casualidad... Que basta la fuerza que tiene un beso para poder matarlos a todos. Un puñal, unas tijeras duran siempre y este pecho mío dura sólo un momento.

CRIADA

[Escuchando] Ahí[35] llega su padre.

NOVIA

[Con sigilo][36] Todos mis trajes de color, los metes en una maleta.

CRIADA

[Temblando] Sí.

NOVIA

Y tienes preparada la llave del garaje.

CRIADA

[Con miedo] ¡Está bien!

[Entra el PADRE DE LA NOVIA. Es un viejo distraído. Lleva unos prismáticos colgados al cuello. Peluca blanca. Cara rosa. Lleva guantes blancos y traje negro. Tiene detalles de una delicada miopía.]

PADRE

¿Estás ya preparada?

FIANCÉE

No.

MAID

The wind will burn your skin.

FIANCÉE

I want it to. I want to turn black. Black as a boy, and not bleed when I fall and not get hurt when I pick a blackberry. Everyone's walking on the tightrope with their eyes closed. And I, I want to have my feet firmly planted on the ground. Last night I dreamed that little children grow just by chance . . . that the power of a kiss could kill them all. A knife, a pair of scissors last forever and this breast of mine lasts just a little while.

MAID

[Listening] Here comes your father.

FIANCÉE

[Surreptitiously] Take all my colored dresses and pack them in a suitcase.

MAID

[Trembling] All right.

FIANCÉE

And have the key to the garage ready.

MAID

[Fearfully] Very well!

> *[Enter the FATHER OF THE FIANCÉE. He is an abstracted old man. A pair of binoculars hang from his neck. White wig. Pink face. He wears white gloves and a black suit. He appears to be a fragile, near-sighted fellow.]*

FATHER

Are you all ready?

NOVIA

[*Irritada*] ¿Pero para qué tengo que estar preparada?

PADRE

¡Que ha llegado!

NOVIA

¿Y qué?

PADRE

Pues que como estás comprometida y se trata de tu vida, de tu felicidad, es natural que estés contenta y decidida.

NOVIA

Pues no estoy.

PADRE

¿Cómo?

NOVIA

Que no estoy contenta, ¿y tú?

PADRE

Pero hija . . . ¿Qué va a decir ese hombre?

NOVIA

¡Que diga lo que quiera!

PADRE

Viene a casarse contigo. Tú le has escrito durante los cinco años que ha durado nuestro viaje. Tú no has bailado con nadie en los trasatlánticos, no te has interesado por nadie. ¿Qué cambio es éste?

NOVIA

No quiero verlo. Es preciso que yo viva. Habla demasiado.

FIANCÉE

[Irritated] And what am I supposed to be ready for?

FATHER

He's here!

FIANCÉE

So what?

FATHER

Well, as you're engaged and we're talking about your whole life, your happiness, it's only natural you should be content and firmly resolved.

FIANCÉE

Well, I'm not.

FATHER

What?

FIANCÉE

I'm not content, are you?

FATHER

But child . . . what's this man going to say?

FIANCÉE

Whatever he pleases!

FATHER

He's come to marry you. You wrote to him the whole five years we were travelling. You wouldn't dance with anyone on the ocean liners, you weren't interested in anyone. What's come over you?

FIANCÉE

I don't want to see him. I need to live. He talks too much.

PADRE

¡Ay! ¿Por qué no lo dijiste antes?

NOVIA

Antes no existía yo tampoco. Existían la tierra y el mar, pero yo dormía dulcemente en los almohadones del tren.

PADRE

Ese hombre me insultará con toda la razón.[37] ¡Ay Dios mío! Ya estaba todo arreglado. Te había regalado el hermoso[38] traje de novia. Ahí dentro está, en el maniquí.

NOVIA

No me hables de esto. No quiero.

PADRE

¿Y yo? ¿Y yo? ¿Es que no tengo derecho a descansar? Esta noche hay un eclipse de luna. Ya no podré mirarlo desde la terraza. En cuanto paso una irritación, se me sube la sangre a los ojos y no veo. ¿Qué hacemos con este hombre?

NOVIA

Lo que tú quieras. Yo no quiero verlo.

PADRE

[Enérgico y sacando fuerzas de voluntad] ¡Tienes que cumplir tu compromiso!

NOVIA

¡No lo cumplo!

PADRE

¡Es preciso!

NOVIA

No.

FATHER

Ah! Why didn't you tell me this before?

FIANCÉE

Before, I didn't exist. The earth and the sea existed, but I just slept sweetly against the cushions in the train.

FATHER

The man will insult me, with good reason. For God's sake! And it was all arranged. He'd already given you a beautiful wedding dress. It's right in there, on the mannequin.

FIANCÉE

Don't talk about it. I don't want to.

FATHER

And me? What about me? Don't I have the right to some peace? Tonight there's an eclipse of the moon. Now I won't get to watch it from the terrace. When I'm upset, the blood goes to my eyes, and I can't see. What do we do with the man?

FIANCÉE

Whatever you please. I don't want to see him.

FATHER

[Emphatically and calling on reserves of willpower] You're going to go through with your engagement!

FIANCÉE

I won't do it!

FATHER

You have to!

FIANCÉE

No.

PADRE

¡Sí! *[Hace intención de pegarla]*

NOVIA

[Fuerte] NO.[39]

PADRE

Todos contra mí. *[Mira al cielo por el balcón abierto]* Ahora empezará el eclipse. ¡Será hermoso![40] *[Se dirige al balcón]* Ya han apagado las lámparas. *[Con angustia]* Lo he estado esperando mucho tiempo. Y ahora ya no lo veo. ¿Por qué lo has engañado?

NOVIA

Yo no lo he engañado.

PADRE

Cinco años día por día. ¡Ay Dios mío!

> *[La CRIADA entra precipitadamente y corre hacia el balcón. Fuera se oyen voces.]*

CRIADA

¡Están discutiendo!

PADRE

¿Quién?

CRIADA

Ya ha entrado. *[Sale rápidamente.]*

PADRE

¿Qué pasa?

NOVIA

¿Dónde vas? *[Con angustia]* ¡Cierra la puerta!

PADRE

¿Pero por qué?

FATHER

Yes! *[Makes as though to strike her]*

FIANCÉE

[Forcefully] NO.

FATHER

Everyone's against me! *[Looks at the sky through the open balcony]* The eclipse is about to begin. It's going to be beautiful! *[Goes to the balcony]* They've doused the lamps. *[Distressed]* I've waited so long for this. And now I'm not going to see it. Why did you deceive him?

FIANCÉE

I haven't deceived him.

FATHER

Five years, day by day. For God's sake!

> *[The MAID enters suddenly and runs to the balcony. Outside, shouts are heard.]*

MAID

They're arguing!

FATHER

Who is?

MAID

He's come in. *[Exits quickly]*

FATHER

What is this?

FIANCÉE

Where are you going? *[Distressed]* Shut the door!

FATHER

But why?

NOVIA

¡Ah!

[Aparece el JOVEN. Viene vestido de calle. Se arregla el cabello. En el momento de entrar se encienden todas las luces de la escena y los ramos de bombillas que llevan los ángeles en la mano. Quedan los tres personajes mirándose quietos y en silencio.]

JOVEN

Perdonen . . .

[Pausa.]

PADRE

[Con embarazo] Siéntese . . .

[Entra la CRIADA muy nerviosa con las manos sobre el pecho.]

JOVEN

[Dando la mano a la NOVIA] ¡Ha sido un viaje tan largo!

NOVIA

[Mirándole muy fija y sin soltarle la mano] Sí. Un viaje frío. Ha nevado mucho estos últimos años. *[Le suelta la mano.]*

JOVEN

Ustedes me perdonarán[41] pero de correr, de subir la escalera, estoy agitado. Y luego . . . en la calle he golpeado a unos niños que estaban matando un gato a pedradas.

[El PADRE le ofrece una silla.]

NOVIA

[A la CRIADA] Una mano fría. Una mano de cera cortada.

CRIADA

¡La va a oir![42]

NOVIA

Y una mirada antigua. Una mirada que se parte como el ala de una mariposa seca.

FIANCÉE

Oh!

[The YOUNG MAN appears, dressed in street clothes. He is fixing his hair. Just as he enters, all the stage lights go up, including the branches of bulbs the angels are holding in their hands. The three characters stand looking at one another, silent and still.]

YOUNG MAN

Excuse me . . . .

[Pause.]

FATHER

[Awkwardly] Please, do sit down . . . .

[Enter the MAID, very nervously, with her hands at her breast.]

YOUNG MAN

[Taking the FIANCÉE's hand] What a long trip it's been!

FIANCÉE

[Looking at him fixedly and without releasing his hand] Yes. A cold trip. It's snowed so much these last few years. *[Releases his hand]*

YOUNG MAN

You'll have to excuse me, but what with running and climbing the stairs, I'm a bit unsettled. And also . . . some children were stoning a cat in the street. I had to beat them.

[The FATHER offers him a chair.]

FIANCÉE

[To the MAID] A cold hand. A severed hand of wax.

MAID

He'll hear you!

FIANCÉE

And old, old eyes. A look that splits in two like the wing of a dried butterfly.

JOVEN

No, no puedo estar sentado. Prefiero charlar...[43] De pronto, mientras subía la escalera, vinieron a mi memoria todas las canciones que había olvidado y las quería cantar todas a la vez. *[Se acerca a la NOVIA]*... Las trenzas...

NOVIA

Nunca tuve trenzas.

JOVEN

Sería la luz de la luna. Sería el aire cuajado en bocas para besar tu cabeza.

> *[La CRIADA se retira a un rincón. El PADRE se asoma a los balcones y mira con los prismáticos.]*

NOVIA

Y tú, ¿no eras más alto?

JOVEN

No.[44]

NOVIA

¿No tenías una sonrisa violenta que era como una garra[45] sobre tu rostro?

JOVEN

No.

NOVIA

¿Y no jugabas tú al rugby?

JOVEN

Nunca.

NOVIA

[Con pasión] ¿Y no llevabas un caballo de las crines y matabas en un día tres mil faisanes?

YOUNG MAN

No, I can't be seated. I'd rather just talk.... Suddenly, as I was climbing the stairs, all the songs I'd ever forgotten came to mind, and I wanted to sing them all at once. *[Approaches the FI-ANCÉE]* ... Your braids....

FIANCÉE

I never had braids.

YOUNG MAN

It must have been the moonlight. It must have been the wind pressed into mouths to kiss your head.

[The MAID withdraws into a corner. The FATHER goes to the balcony and looks out through his binoculars.]

FIANCÉE

What about you? Weren't you taller?

YOUNG MAN

No.

FIANCÉE

And didn't you have a wicked smile like a claw on your face?

YOUNG MAN

No.

FIANCÉE

And didn't you play football?

YOUNG MAN

Not once.

FIANCÉE

[Passionately] And didn't you take a horse by the mane and kill three thousand pheasants in a single day?

JOVEN

Jamás.

NOVIA

¡Entonces! ¿A qué vienes a buscarme? Tenía las manos llenas de anillos. ¿Dónde hay una gota de sangre?

JOVEN

Yo la derramaré si te gusta.

NOVIA

[Enérgica][46] No es tu sangre, ¡es la mía!

JOVEN

¡Ahora nadie podrá[47] separar mis brazos de tu cuello!

NOVIA

No son tus brazos, son los míos. Soy yo la que se quiere quemar en otro fuego.

JOVEN

No hay más fuego que el mío. *[La abraza]* Porque te he esperado y ahora gano mi sueño. Y no son sueño tus trenzas porque las haré yo mismo de tu cabello, ni es sueño tu cintura donde canta la sangre mía, porque es mía esta sangre, ganada[48] lentamente a través de una lluvia y mío este sueño.

NOVIA

[Desasiéndose][49] ¡Déjame! Todo lo podías haber dicho menos la palabra sueño. Yo no quiero soñar. Aquí no se sueña.[50]

JOVEN

¡Pero se ama!

NOVIA

Tampoco se ama. ¡Vete!

YOUNG MAN

Never.

FIANCÉE

Well then? What are you doing here with me? My hands were full of rings. Where is there a drop of blood?

YOUNG MAN

I'll bleed, if it pleases you.

FIANCÉE

[Emphatically] Not your blood! Mine!

YOUNG MAN

Now no one will be able to take my arms from around your neck!

FIANCÉE

Not your arms! Mine! It's me that wants to burn in another fire.

YOUNG MAN

There is no fire but mine. *[Embraces her]* Because I waited for you, and now I win my dream. And your braids are no dream, because I'll weave them myself with your hair, and your waist where my blood sings is no dream, because this blood is mine, won slowly through the long rain and mine is all this dream.

FIANCÉE

[Disengaging herself] Let me go! You could have said anything but dream. I don't want to dream. Nobody dreams here.

YOUNG MAN

But somebody loves!

FIANCÉE

Nobody loves either. Go away!

JOVEN

[Aterrado] ¿Qué dices?

NOVIA

Que busques otra mujer a quien puedas hacerle trenzas.

JOVEN

[Como despertando] ¡NO![51]

NOVIA

¿Cómo voy a dejar que entres en mi alcoba cuando ya ha entrado otro?

JOVEN

¡Ay! *[Se cubre la cara con las manos]*

NOVIA

Dos días tan sólo han bastado para sentirme cargada de cadenas. En los espejos y entre los encajes de la cama oigo ya el gemido de un niño que me persigue.[52]

JOVEN

Pero mi casa está ya levantada. Con muros que yo mismo he tocado. ¿Voy a dejar que la viva el aire?

NOVIA

¿Y qué culpa tengo yo? ¿Quieres que me vaya contigo?

JOVEN

[Sentándose en una silla, abatido] Sí, sí, vente.

NOVIA

Un espejo, una mesa estarían más cerca de tí que yo.[53]

JOVEN

¿Qué voy a hacer ahora?[54]

YOUNG MAN

[Stricken] What are you saying?

FIANCÉE

Go find another woman to make braids for.

YOUNG MAN

[As though awakening] NO!

FIANCÉE

How shall I have you in my bedroom when another has come here before you?

YOUNG MAN

Oh! *[Covers his face with his hands]*

FIANCÉE

Just two days, and already I feel loaded with chains. I hear the cry of a child following me in the mirrors and the bed's lace.

YOUNG MAN

But my house is all built. I've felt the walls with my own hands. Who's going to live in it, the wind?

FIANCÉE

And is that my fault? You want me to go with you?

YOUNG MAN

[Sitting down in a chair, dejected] Yes, yes, come.

FIANCÉE

A mirror, a table would be closer to you than I would.

YOUNG MAN

What do I do now?

NOVIA

Amar.

JOVEN

¿A quién?

NOVIA

Busca. Por las calles, por el campo . . .

JOVEN

[Enérgico] No busco. Te tengo a tí. Estás aquí, entre mis manos, en este mismo instante y no me puedes cerrar la puerta, porque vengo mojado por una lluvia de cinco años. Y porque después no hay nada, porque después no puedo amar, porque después se ha acabado todo.

NOVIA

¡Suelta!

JOVEN

No es tu engaño lo que me duele. Tú no eres nada.[55] Tú no significas nada. Es mi tesoro perdido, es mi amor sin objeto. ¡Pero vendrás!

NOVIA

¡No iré!

JOVEN

Para que no tenga que volver a empezar. Siento que se me olvidan hasta las letras.

NOVIA

No iré.

JOVEN

Para que no muera, ¿lo oyes?, ¡para que no muera!

FIANCÉE

Love.

YOUNG MAN

Who?

FIANCÉE

Look. Look in the streets, look in the fields . . . .

YOUNG MAN

[Emphatic] No, I won't look. I have you. You're here, in my hands, this very instant, and you can't shut the door on me, because I'm wet with five years' rain. And because then there is nothing, then I can't love, then it's all over.

FIANCÉE

Let go of me!

YOUNG MAN

It isn't your deceit that hurts. You are nothing. You mean nothing. It's my lost treasure, my purposeless love. But you will come!

FIANCÉE

I will not!

YOUNG MAN

So I don't have to start all over again. I feel as though I were forgetting even how to talk.

FIANCÉE

I won't go.

YOUNG MAN

So I don't die, do you hear me? So I don't die!

NOVIA

¡Déjame!

CRIADA

[Saliendo][56] ¡Señorita! ¡Señor![57]

[El JOVEN suelta a la NOVIA.]

PADRE

[Entrando] ¿Quién grita?[58]

NOVIA

Nadie.

PADRE

[Mirando al JOVEN] Caballero . . .

JOVEN

[Abatido] Hablábamos . . .

NOVIA

[Al PADRE] Es preciso que le devuelva los regalos . . . *[El JOVEN hace un movimiento]* Todos. Sería injusto . . . Todos . . ., menos los abanicos . . ., porque se han roto.

JOVEN

[Recordando] Dos abanicos.

NOVIA

Uno azul . . .

JOVEN

Con tres góndolas hundidas . . .

NOVIA

Y otro blanco . . .

FIANCÉE

Leave me alone!

MAID

[Entering] Miss! Sir!

> *[The YOUNG MAN releases the FIANCÉE.]*

FATHER

[Entering] Who's shouting?

FIANCÉE

No one.

FATHER

[Looking at the YOUNG MAN] My dear sir . . . .

YOUNG MAN

[Dejected] We were speaking . . . .

FIANCÉE

[To the FATHER] You must return his gifts . . . . *[The YOUNG MAN reacts.]* All of them. It would be wrong . . . all of them . . . , except for the fans . . . , since they're broken.

YOUNG MAN

[Remembering] Two fans.

FIANCÉE

One blue . . . .

YOUNG MAN

With three sunken gondolas . . . .

FIANCÉE

And the other white . . . .

JOVEN

Que tenía en el centro la cabeza de un tigre. Y . . . , ¿están rotos?

CRIADA

Las últimas varillas se las llevó el niño[59] del carbonero.

PADRE

Eran unos abanicos buenos,[60] pero vamos . . .

JOVEN

[Sonriendo] No importa que se hayan perdido. Me hacen ahora mismo un aire que me quema la piel.

CRIADA

[A la NOVIA] ¿También el traje de novia?

NOVIA

Está claro.

CRIADA

[Llorosa] Ahí dentro está, en el maniquí.[61]

PADRE

[Al JOVEN] Yo quisiera que . . .

JOVEN

No importa.[62]

PADRE

De todos modos está usted en su casa.

JOVEN

¡Gracias!

PADRE

[Que mira siempre al balcón] Debe estar ya en el comienzo.[63] Usted perdone . . . [A la NOVIA] ¿Vienes? . . .

YOUNG MAN

It had a tiger's face in the middle, and . . . they're broken?

MAID

The coal man's boy took the last sticks.

FATHER

They were good fans, but we'll . . . .

YOUNG MAN

[*Smiling*] It doesn't matter that they're gone. Right this minute, the wind of them burns my skin.

MAID

[*To the FIANCÉE*] The wedding dress too?

FIANCÉE

Of course.

MAID

[*Tearfully*] It's right in there, on the mannequin.

FATHER

[*To the YOUNG MAN*] If only I could . . . .

YOUNG MAN

It doesn't matter.

FATHER

At any rate, please make yourself at home. Our house is your house.

YOUNG MAN

Thank you!

FATHER

[*Who is looking always towards the balcony*] It ought to have started already. Excuse us . . . . [*To the FIANCÉE*] Are you coming?

NOVIA

Sí. *[Al JOVEN]* ¡Adiós!

JOVEN

¡Adiós!

[Salen.]

VOZ

[Fuera] ¡Adiós!

JOVEN

Adiós..., ¿y qué? ¿Qué hago con esta hora que viene y que no conozco? ¿Dónde voy?

[La luz de la escena se oscurece. Las bombillas de los ángeles toman una luz azul. Por los balcones vuelve a entrar una luz de luna que irá[64] en aumento hasta el final.]

[Se oye un gemido.]

JOVEN

[Mirando a la puerta] ¿Quién?

[Entra en escena EL VESTIDO DE NOVIA. Este personaje tiene la cara gris, las cejas y los labios dorados, como un MANIQUI de escaparate de lujo. Lleva peluca y guantes de oro. Trae puesto con cierto embarazo un espléndido traje de novia blanco, con larga cola y velo.][65]

MANIQUI

[Canta y llora]

    ¿Quién usará la ropa[66] buena
de la novia chiquita y morena?
Mi cola se pierde por el mar.
Y la luna lleva puesta mi corona de azahar.
Mi anillo, ¡señor!, mi anillo de oro viejo.
¡Se hundió por las arenas del espejo!
¿Quién se pondrá mi traje? ¿Quién se lo pondrá?
Se lo pondrá la ría grande para casarse con el mar.

FIANCÉE

Yes. *[To the YOUNG MAN]* Goodbye!

YOUNG MAN

Goodbye!

[They exit.]

VOICE

[Off] Goodbye!

YOUNG MAN

Goodbye . . . , and then what? What is this hour that's come? I don't recognize it. What do I do with it? Where do I go?

[The stage lights dim. The bulbs in the angels' hands take on a blue light. Moonlight comes in again through the balconies, increasing until the end of the act.]

[Sound of a wail.]

YOUNG MAN

[Looking towards the door] Who?

[The WEDDING DRESS enters on the stage. This character has a gray face, its lips and eyebrows gilded, like a MANNEQUIN in a fancy store window. Its wig and gloves are golden. It is wearing, somewhat awkwardly, a splendid white wedding dress with a long train and veil.]

MANNEQUIN

[Sings and cries]

Who'll use these lovely clothes so white,
if not the little dark-haired bride?
The sea swallows the train of my gown
and the moon puts on my orange-blossom crown.
My ring, dear sir, my old, old golden ring!
It sank in the mirror's sand, whispering!
Who'll wear my wedding dress, who'll wear it for me?
The river's mouth will wear it to marry the sea.

JOVEN

¿Qué cantas, díme?

MANIQUI

     Yo canto
muerte que no tuve nunca,
dolor de velo sin uso
con llanto de seda y pluma.
Ropa interior que se queda
helada de nieve oscura
sin que los encajes puedan
competir con las espumas.
Telas que cubren la carne
serán para el agua turbia
y en vez de rumor caliente
quebrado torso de lluvia.

¿Quién usará la ropa buena
de la novia chiquita y morena?

JOVEN

Se la pondrá el aire oscuro
jugando al alba en su gruta,
ligas de raso los juncos,
medias de seda la luna.
Dale el velo a las arañas
para que coman y cubran
las palomas, enredadas
en sus hilos de hermosura.
Nadie se pondrá tu traje,
forma blanca y luz confusa,
que seda y escarcha fueron
livianas arquitecturas.

MANIQUI

Mi cola se pierde por el mar.

JOVEN

Y la luna lleva[67] en vilo tu corona de azahar.

YOUNG MAN

What is that you're singing?

MANNEQUIN

                  I sing
a death that was never my own,
the pain of a now useless veil,
a long cry of silk and of down.
A bodice that always will be
frozen in the shadow of the snow,
its lace simply unable to
shine brighter than the white sea foam.
The cloth that should cover her flesh
on the rolling waters will flow
and instead of the warm touch of her,
the rain with its broken torso.

Who'll use these lovely clothes so white,
if not the little dark-haired bride?

YOUNG MAN

The shadow wind will put them on
playing at dawn in its grotto,
the satin garters for the reeds
and silk stockings for the moonglow.
Let the spiders have the white veil
to tangle the doves in its folds,
to wrap them up and eat them there,
helpless in the beautiful cloth.
No one's going to put on your dress,
white shape and light that sparkles so,
for silk and frost are built so frail
they vanish as quickly as smoke.

MANNEQUIN

The sea swallows the train of my gown.

YOUNG MAN

And the moon lifts off your orange-blossom crown.

MANIQUI

[Irritado]

¡No quiero! Mis sedas tienen
hilo a hilo y una a una
ansia de calor de boda.[68]
Y mi camisa pregunta
dónde están las manos tibias
que oprimen en la cintura.

JOVEN

Yo también pregunto. Calla.

MANIQUI

Mientes. Tú tienes la culpa.
Pudiste ser para mí
potro de plomo y espuma
el aire roto en el freno
y el mar atado en la grupa.
Pudiste ser un relincho
y eres dormida laguna
con hojas secas y musgo
donde este traje se pudra.
Mi anillo, ¡señor!, mi anillo de oro viejo.

JOVEN

¡Se hundió por las arenas del espejo!

MANIQUI

¿Por qué no viniste antes?[69]
Ella esperaba desnuda
como una sierpe de viento
desmayada por las puntas.

JOVEN

[Levantándose]

Silencio. Déjame. Vete.
O te romperé con furia
las iniciales de nardo
que la blanca seda oculta.

MANNEQUIN

[Irritated]

No, I won't let it! Thread by thread
and one by one, my silken clothes
all want the heat of a wedding.
And my shirtwaist wants to know
where are the warm and searching hands
to close around its waist below.

YOUNG MAN

I too want to know. Be quiet.

MANNEQUIN

You're lying! It's all because you won't.
For me you could have been
an iron horse, a colt of foam,
the wind broken on your bridle
and the sea bound to your hipbone.
You could have been a shaking mane,
and you're only a pond, still and old,
dry leaves and moss all around you
where this dress of mine gathers mold.
My ring, dear sir, my old, old golden ring!

YOUNG MAN

It sank in the mirror's sand, whispering!

MANNEQUIN

Why didn't you come before this?
She waited there naked as though
she were a serpent of the wind
fainted on her lacy pillow.

YOUNG MAN

[Rising]

Quiet. Let me be. Go away.
I'll be so angry if you don't
I'll tear the monogram of nard
concealed in white silk at your throat.

Vete a la calle a buscar
hombros de virgen nocturna
o guitarras que te lloren
seis largos gritos de música.

MANIQUI
Te seguiré siempre.

JOVEN
                    ¡Nunca!

MANIQUI
¡Déjame hablarte!

JOVEN
                    ¡Es inútil!
¡No quiero saber!

MANIQUI
                    Escucha.
Mira.

JOVEN
        ¿Qué?

MANIQUI
                Un trajecito
que robé de la costura.
[Enseña un traje rosa de niño.]
Dos fuentes[70] de leche blanca
mojan mis sedas de angustia
y un dolor blanco de abejas[71]
cubre de rayos mi nuca.
¡Mi hijo! ¡Quiero a mi hijo!

Go look on the street if you want
some night virgin's shoulder to cloak
or guitars to wail you a music
in six long wavering notes.

MANNEQUIN
I'll follow you always.

YOUNG MAN
                              No, you won't!

MANNEQUIN
Let me speak to you!

YOUNG MAN
                              It's useless!

MANNEQUIN
Listen!

YOUNG MAN
          I don't want to know!

MANNEQUIN
Look here.

YOUNG MAN
          What is it?

MANNEQUIN
                              A little suit
that I stole from the room where they sew.
[Holds up a child's pink suit.]
Two streams of white milk flow from me
with a sorrow that soaks my silk robes,
and a white pain of honeybees
covers my neck in lightning bolts.
My son! I want to have my son!

Por mi falda lo dibujan
estas cintas que me estallan
de alegría en la cintura.
¡Y es tu hijo!

JOVEN

[Coge el trajecito][72]
                    Sí, mi hijo:
donde llegan y se juntan
pájaros de sueño loco
y jazmines de cordura.

[Angustiado]

¿Y si mi niño no llega,
pájaro que el aire cruza
no puede cantar?[73]

MANIQUI

                    No puede.

JOVEN

¿Y si mi niño no llega,
velero que el agua surca
no puede nadar?

MANIQUI

                    No puede.

JOVEN

Quieta el arpa de la lluvia,
un mar hecho piedra ríe
últimas olas oscuras.

MANIQUI

¿Quién se pondrá mi traje? ¿Quién se lo pondrá?

JOVEN

[Entusiasmado y rotundo]

Se lo pondrá mujer[74] que espera, por las orillas de la mar.

These ribbons on my skirts explode
with joy because they're picturing
the shape of him beneath my clothes.
And he is your son!

YOUNG MAN

[Taking the little suit]
Yes, my son:
where the birds of a wild dream go
to meet the jasmines of goodness.

[In anguish]
And if my child should never grow?
A bird that's flying through the air,
can it sing as it flies?

MANNEQUIN

No, no.

YOUNG MAN

And if my child should never grow?
A boat that skims across the water,
can it swim as it sails?

MANNEQUIN

No, no.

YOUNG MAN

The harp of the rain is silent,
the last waves are laughing shadows
in a sea that has turned to stone.

MANNEQUIN

Who'll wear my wedding dress? Who'll wear it for me?

YOUNG MAN

[Enthusiastic and positive]
The woman will wear it who waits, beside the sea.

MANIQUI

Te espera siempre, ¿recuerdas?
Estaba en tu casa oculta.
Ella te amaba y se fué.
Tu niño canta en su cuna
y, como es niño de nieve,
espera la sangre tuya.
Corre, a buscarla, ¡deprisa!
Y entrégamela desnuda,[75]
para que mis sedas puedan
hilo a hilo y una a una
abrir la rosa que cubre
en vientre[76] de carne rubia.

JOVEN

He de vivir.

MANIQUI

　　　　　¡Sin espera!

JOVEN

Mi niño canta en su cuna
y, como es niño de nieve,
aguarda calor y ayuda.

MANIQUI

[Por el traje del niño][77]
　　¡Dáme el traje!

JOVEN

[Dulce]　　　　　NO.[78]

MANIQUI

[Arrebatándoselo]　　　　¡Lo quiero!
　　Mientras tú vences y buscas
yo cantaré una canción
sobre sus[79] tiernas arrugas.*[Lo besa.]*

MANNEQUIN

Remember her? She always waits.
She stayed unnoticed in your home.
She loved you, and she had to go.
Your child is still a child of snow,
but he sings inside his cradle,
waits for your blood to be his own.
Go now, go quickly and find her,
and bring her naked to me, so
that thread by thread and one by one
my silken clothes may open the rose
that is concealed there inside her,
in her belly as blonde as gold.

YOUNG MAN

I have to live.

MANNEQUIN

No more waiting!

YOUNG MAN

My child is still a child of snow,
but he sings inside his cradle.
He needs my heat, my help to grow.

MANNEQUIN

[Referring to the child's clothes]
Give me the suit!

YOUNG MAN

[Sweetly]   NO.

MANNEQUIN

[Grabbing it from him]   I want it!
While you go to win her for your own,
I'll stay and sing a lullabye
to the tender folds in the clothes.*[Kisses them.]*

JOVEN

¡Pronto! ¿Dónde está?

MANIQUI

En la calle.

JOVEN

Antes que la roja luna
limpie con sangre de eclipse
la perfección de su curva,
traeré temblando de amor
mi propia mujer desnuda...

[La luz es de un azul intenso. Entra la CRIADA por la izquierda con un candelabro y la escena toma suavemente su luz normal[80] sin descuidar la luz azul de los balcones abiertos de par en par que hay en el fondo. En el momento que aparece[81] la CRIADA, el MA- NIQUI queda rígido con una postura de escaparate. La cabeza inclinada y las manos levantadas en actitud delicadísima. La CRIADA deja el candelabro sobre la mesa del tocador, siempre en actitud compungida, y mirando al JOVEN. En este momento aparece el VIEJO por una puerta de la derecha. La luz crece.][82]

JOVEN

[Asombrado] ¡Usted!

VIEJO

[Da muestras de una gran agitación y se lleva las manos al pecho. Trae[83] un pañuelo de seda en la mano.] ¡Sí! ¡Yo!

[La CRIADA sale rápidamente por un balcón.][84]

JOVEN

[Agrio] No me hace ninguna falta.

VIEJO

Más que nunca. ¡Ay! ¡Me has herido! ¿Por qué subiste? Yo sabía lo que iba a pasar. ¡Ay!

JOVEN

[Acercándose,[85] dulce] ¿Qué le pasa?

YOUNG MAN

Right now! Where is she?

MANNEQUIN

In the streets.

YOUNG MAN

Before the moon can wash its bowl
in the dark blood of an eclipse
and show its perfect curve once more,
I'll bring you here, trembling with love,
a naked woman of my own . . . .

[The light is intensely blue. Enter the MAID with a candelabra from left, and the stage gradually returns to its normal light, but without losing the blue light that comes in through the wide-open balconies at rear. As soon as the MAID appears, the MANNE-QUIN goes rigid in a store-window pose, the head inclined and the hands raised in an attitude of extreme delicacy. The MAID leaves the candelabra on the dressing table, looking remorseful all the while, and glancing at the YOUNG MAN. Just then, the OLD MAN appears through a door at right. The light goes up.]

YOUNG MAN

[Startled] You!

OLD MAN

[He seems very agitated, holding his hands to his chest. There is a silk handkerchief in his hand.] Yes! Me!

[The MAID exits quickly through a balcony.]

YOUNG MAN

[Sourly] I don't need you anymore.

OLD MAN

More than ever. Oh! You hurt me! Why did you have to climb the stairs? I knew what would happen. Oh!

YOUNG MAN

[Going to him, sweetly] What's the matter?

VIEJO

[Enérgico] Nada. No me pasa nada. Una herida, pero . . . , la sangre se seca y lo pasado, pasado.[86]

[El JOVEN inicia el mutis] ¿Dónde vas?

JOVEN

[Con alegría] ¡A buscar!

VIEJO

¿A quién?

JOVEN

A la mujer que me quiere. Usted la vió en mi casa, ¿no recuerda?

VIEJO

[Severo][87] No recuerdo. Pero espera.

JOVEN

¡No! Ahora mismo. *[El VIEJO le coge del brazo]*

PADRE

[Entrando] ¡Hija! ¿Dónde estás? ¡Hija!

> *[Se oye el cláxon del automóvil.]*

CRIADA

[En el balcón] ¡Señorita! ¡Señorita!

PADRE

[Yéndose al balcón] Hija, ¡espera!, ¡espera! *[Sale.]*

JOVEN

¡Yo también me voy! ¡Yo busco como ella la nueva flor de mi sangre! *[Sale corriendo.]*

VIEJO

¡Espera! ¡Espera! ¡No me dejes herido! ¡Espera![88]

OLD MAN

[Emphatically] Nothing. Nothing's the matter. I'm hurt, but..., blood dries, and what's past is past. *[The YOUNG MAN begins to exit]* Where are you going?

YOUNG MAN

[Brightly] To look for her!

OLD MAN

For who?

YOUNG MAN

For the woman who loves me. You saw her once in my house, don't you remember?

OLD MAN

[Sternly] I don't remember. But wait.

YOUNG MAN

No! Right now. *[The OLD MAN takes him by the arm.]*

FATHER

[Entering] My child! Where are you? My child!

[The car horn honks.]

MAID

[On the balcony] Miss! Miss!

FATHER

[Going to the balcony] My child, wait! Wait! *[Exits.]*

YOUNG MAN

I'm going too! Like her, I'm looking for, the new flower of my blood! *[Exits running.]*

OLD MAN

Wait! Wait! Don't leave me here hurt! Wait!

[Sale. Sus voces de "espera, espera" se pierden por los balcones.[89]* La CRIADA entra rapidísimamente, coge el candelabro y sale por el balcón. Se oye lejano el cláxon. Queda la escena azul y el MANIQUI avanza dolorido. Con dos expresiones. Pregunta en el primer verso con ímpetu y respuesta en el segundo como muy lejana.]*[90]

MANIQUI

Mi anillo, ¡señor!, mi anillo de oro viejo.

[Pausa]

¡Se hundió por las arenas del espejo!

¿Quién se pondrá mi traje? ¿Quién se lo pondrá?

[Pausa]

[Llorando]

Se lo pondrá la ría grande para casarse con el mar.

[Se desmaya y queda tendido en el sofá.]

VOZ

[Fuera] ¡Esperaaa!*[91]*

Telón rápido

Acto Tercero[1]

Bosque. Grandes troncos. En el centro un teatro rodeado de cortinas barrocas con el telón echado. Una escalera[2] une el tabladillo con el escenario. Al levantarse el telón cruzan entre los troncos dos figuras vestidas de negro con las caras blancas de yeso y las manos también blancas. Suena una música lejana. Sale el ARLEQUIN. Viste de negro y verde. Lleva dos caretas, una en cada mano y ocultas en la espalda. Acciona de modo rítmico,[3] como un bailarín.

ARLEQUIN

El Sueño va sobre el Tiempo
flotando como un velero.
Nadie puede abrir semillas
en el corazón del Sueño.

[Se pone una careta de alegrísima expresión.]

¡Ay cómo canta el alba!, ¡cómo canta!

[Exit. His cries of "wait, wait!" are lost among the balconies. Enter the MAID very quickly. She takes the candelabra and exits through the balcony. The horn honks in the distance. The stage turns blue and the MANNEQUIN comes forward, sorrowing. With two different expressions. In the first verse, it asks forcefully, and in the second, it answers as though very distant.]

MANNEQUIN

My ring, dear sir, my old, old golden ring!

[Pause]

It sank in the mirror's sand, whispering.

Who'll wear my wedding dress? Who'll wear it for me?

[Pause]

[Crying]

The river's mouth will wear it, to marry the sea.

[It faints and falls stretched out on the sofa.]

VOICES OF FATHER AND OLD MAN

[Off] Waaaaait!

Fast curtain

Act Three

Forest. Great tree trunks. At center, a theater surrounded in baroque curtains, drawn closed. Stairs join the smaller stage to the larger. As the main curtain rises, two figures dressed in black—with plaster-white faces and white hands—cross among the tree trunks. Sound of distant music. Enter the HARLEQUIN, dressed in black and green. He carries two masks, one in either hand, hiding them behind his back. He moves rhythmically, like a dancer.

HARLEQUIN

Oh Dream travels on over Time.
It floats like a ship on the sea.
And no one can make a seed burst
in the heart of the sailing Dream.

[He puts on a mask with a joyful face.]

Oh and how the dawn sings, how it's singing!

¡Qué témpanos de hielo azul levanta!

[Se la quita.]

El Tiempo va sobre el Sueño
hundido hasta los cabellos.
Ayer y mañana comen
oscuras flores de duelo.

[Se pone una careta de expresión dormida.]

¡Ay cómo canta la noche!, ¡cómo canta!
¡Qué espesura de anémonas levanta!

[Se la quita.]

Sobre la misma columna,
abrazados Sueño y Tiempo
cruza[4] el gemido del niño,
la lengua rota del viejo.

[Con una careta]

¡Ay cómo canta el alba!, ¡cómo canta!

[Con la otra careta]

¡Qué espesura de anémonas levanta!

Y si el Sueño finge muros[5]
en la llanura del Tiempo,
el Tiempo le hace creer
que nace en aquel momento.

¡Ay cómo canta la noche!, ¡cómo canta!
¡Qué témpanos de hielo azul levanta!

[Desde este momento se oirá en el fondo durante todo el acto y con medidos intervalos unas lejanas[6] trompas graves de caza. Aparece una MUCHACHA vestida de negro con túnica griega. Viene saltando con una guirnalda.]

MUCHACHA

¿Quién lo dice?
¿Quién lo dirá?[7]
Mi amante me aguarda
en el fondo del mar.

ARLEQUIN

[Gracioso]

Mentira.

What lovely blue icebergs it's bringing!
[He takes it off.]
> Oh Time travels on over Dream,
> sunk in it up to its hair.
> And yesterday and tomorrow eat
> the shadowy flowers of despair.

[He puts on a mask with a sleeping face.]
> Oh and how the night sings, how it's singing!
> What a mass of windflowers it's bringing!

[He takes it off.]
> On a pillar that's one and the same
> where Dream and Time are embraced
> the wailing cry of a boy
> meets the old man's broken rage.

[With one mask]
> Oh and how the dawn sings, how it's singing!

[With the other mask]
> What a mass of windflowers it's bringing!

> And if on the flatlands of Time,
> Dream pretends there's a fort,
> then Time makes him believe that
> his new dream has just then been born.

> Oh and how the night sings, how it's singing!
> What lovely blue icebergs it's bringing!

[From now on through the whole act, distant mournful hunting horns will sound at measured intervals. A GIRL appears, dressed in a black Greek tunic. She skips rope using a garland.]

GIRL
> Oh who could believe it?
> Oh who could believe?
> My love waits for me
> at the bottom of the sea.

HARLEQUIN
[Teasingly]
> It's a lie!

MUCHACHA

Verdad.
Perdí mi deseo,
perdí mi dedal
y en los troncos grandes
los volví a encontrar.

ARLEQUIN

[Irónico]

Una cuerda muy larga.

MUCHACHA

Larga; para bajar[8]
tiburones y peces
y ramos de coral.

ARLEQUIN

Abajo está.

MUCHACHA

[En voz baja][9]

Muy bajo.

ARLEQUIN

Dormido.

MUCHACHA

¡Abajo está!
Banderas de agua verde
lo nombran capitán.[10]

ARLEQUIN

[En alta voz y gracioso]

¡Mentira!

MUCHACHA

[En alta voz]

Verdad.

GIRL

Truly!
My love and my thimble,
oh where could they be?
I found them again
in the trunks of the trees.

HARLEQUIN

[Ironic]

Such a very long rope.

GIRL

Long enough to take me
to the sharks and the fish
and the fronds of seaweed.

HARLEQUIN

He's way down deep.

GIRL

[In a soft voice]

Way down.

HARLEQUIN

Asleep.

GIRL

He's way down deep!
The flags of green water
have made him their chief.

HARLEQUIN

[Out loud and charmingly]

It's a lie!

GIRL

[Out loud]

Truly!

Perdí mi corona,
perdí mi dedal
y a la media vuelta
los volví a encontrar.

ARLEQUIN

Ahora mismo.

MUCHACHA

¿Ahora?

ARLEQUIN

Tu amante verás
a la media vuelta
del viento y el mar.

MUCHACHA

[Asustada]

Mentira.

ARLEQUIN

Verdad.
Yo te lo daré.

MUCHACHA

[Inquieta]

No me lo darás.
No se llega nunca
al fondo del mar.

ARLEQUIN

[A voces y como si estuviera en el circo]

¡Señor hombre acuda!

[Aparece un espléndido PAYASO lleno de lentejuelas. Su cabeza empolvada dará sensación de calavera. Ríe a grandes carcajadas.]

My crown and my thimble,
oh where could they be?
I found them again
when I turned round to see.

HARLEQUIN

Right now then.

GIRL

Right now?

HARLEQUIN

Your lover you'll see
when you turn halfway round
to the wind and the sea.

GIRL

[Afraid]

It's a lie!

HARLEQUIN

Truly!
I'll give him to you.

GIRL

[Disturbed]

You can't give him to me.
No one can get to
the bottom of the sea.

HARLEQUIN

[Shouting, as though he were in the circus]

Appear, Mister Man!

[A splendid, spangled CLOWN appears. His powdered head gives
the impression of a skull. He laughs in great bursts.]

ARLEQUIN

Usted le dará
a esta muchachita...

PAYASO

Su novio del mar.[11]

[Se remanga]

Venga una escalera.

MUCHACHA

[Asustada]

¿Sí?

PAYASO

[A la MUCHACHA]

Para bajar.

[Al fondo][12]

¡Buenas noches!

ARLEQUIN

¡Bravo!

PAYASO

[Al ARLEQUIN]

¡Tú mira hacia allá!

[El ARLEQUIN riendo se vuelve.]

¡Vamos toca! *[Palmotea]*

ARLEQUIN

Toco.[13]

[El ARLEQUIN toca un violín blanco con dos cuerdas de oro. Debe ser grande y plano.][14]

PAYASO

[Lleva el compás con la cabeza] ¡Lindo![15]

[Canta] Novio ¿dónde estás?[16]

HARLEQUIN
It's your job to bring
this sweet little girl . . . .

CLOWN
To her man in the sea.
[Rolls up his sleeves]
Yes, yes. A ladder, please.

GIRL
[Afraid]
Yes?

CLOWN
[To the GIRL]
To go down deep.
[To the depths, towards the audience]
Good evening!

HARLEQUIN
Bravo!

CLOWN
[To the HARLEQUIN]
You, look off over there!
[Laughing, the HARLEQUIN turns around.]
Now play! *[He claps]*

HARLEQUIN
I'm playing.
*[The HARLEQUIN plays on a white violin with two gold strings.
It should be large and flat.]*

CLOWN
[Keeps time with his head] Sweet!
[Sings] Oh bridegroom, where can you be?

ARLEQUIN

[Fingiendo la voz][17]

> Por las frescas algas
> yo voy a cazar
> grandes caracolas
> y lirios de sal.

MUCHACHA

[Gritando[18] asustada de la realidad]

> ¡No quiero!

PAYASO

> ¡Silencio!

[El ARLEQUIN se ríe.][19]

MUCHACHA

[Al PAYASO con miedo]

> Me voy a saltar
> por las hierbas altas.[20]

ARLEQUIN

[Jocoso y volviéndose][21]

> ¡Mentira!

MUCHACHA

> Verdad.

[Al PAYASO][22]

> Luego nos iremos
> al agua del mar.

[Inicia el mutis llorando.]

> ¿Quién lo dice?
> ¿Quién lo dirá?
> Perdí mi corona
> Perdí mi dedal.

HARLEQUIN

[Affecting another voice]
> Through the branches of coral
> I hunt and I seek
> the great sea snails
> and the salt's lilies.

GIRL

[Crying out, afraid of the reality]
> I don't want to!

CLOWN

> Silence!

[The HARLEQUIN laughs.]

GIRL

[Fearfully, to the CLOWN]
> I'd rather skip free
> through the tall waving grass.

HARLEQUIN

[Facetiously and turning around]
> It's a lie!

GIRL

> Truly!

[To the CLOWN]
> Some other time we'll pass
> through the water of the sea.

[She begins her exit, crying.]
> Oh who could believe it?
> Oh who could believe?
> My crown and my thimble,
> Oh where could they be?

ARLEQUIN

[Melancólico]

> A la media vuelta
> del viento y el mar.

[Sale la MUCHACHA.]

PAYASO

[Señalando]

> Allí.

ARLEQUIN

> ¿Dónde?, ¿a qué?

PAYASO

> A representar:
> Un niño pequeño
> que quiere cambiar
> en flores de acero
> su trozo de pan.

ARLEQUIN

[Levemente incrédulo][23]

> Mentira.

PAYASO

[Severo]

> Verdad.
> Perdí rosa y curva,
> perdí mi collar
> y en marfil reciente
> los volví a encontrar.[24]

ARLEQUIN

[Adoptando una actitud de circo y a voces,[25] como si los oyera el niño.]

> ¡Señor hombre! ¡Venga![26] *[Inicia el mutis]*

HARLEQUIN

[Melancholy]

> Turned halfway round
> in the wind and the sea.

[The GIRL exits.]

CLOWN

[Pointing]

> Over there.

HARLEQUIN

> Where? What for?

CLOWN

> To perform, silly:
> A certain little boy
> who would like to see
> his pieces of bread
> turned to flowers of steel.

HARLEQUIN

[Slightly doubtful]

> It's a lie!

CLOWN

[Sternly]

> Truly!
> My rose, curve and necklace,
> oh where could they be?
> I found them again
> in the fresh ivory.

HARLEQUIN

[Adopting a circus pose and shouting, as though for the boy to hear.]
> Mister Man! Come forward! *[Begins exit]*

PAYASO

[A voces y mirando al bosque y adelantándose al ARLEQUIN.]
No tanto gritar.
¡Buenos días!

[En voz baja]

¡Vamos!

[En alta voz][27]
Toca.

ARLEQUIN

¿Toco?

PAYASO

Un vals.

[El ARLEQUIN empieza a tocar.]
[En voz baja][28]
¡Deprisa!

[En alta voz]
Señores:
voy a demostrar . . .

ARLEQUIN

Que en marfil reciente[29]
los volvió a encontrar.

PAYASO

Voy a demostrar . . . *[Sale]*

ARLEQUIN

[Saliendo]
La rueda que gira
del viento y el mar.

[Se oyen las trompas. Sale la MECANOGRAFA. Viste un traje de tenis, con boina de color intenso. Encima del vestido una capa larga de una sola gasa.[30] Viene con la MASCARA 1. Esta viste un traje amarillo rabioso de 1900 con larga cola, [31] pelo de seda

CLOWN

[Shouting and looking towards the forest and getting ahead of the HARLE-QUIN.]
    You don't have to scream!
    Good day!

[In a soft voice]
          Let's go!

[Out loud]
    Play.

HARLEQUIN
    Play what?

CLOWN
          A waltz.

[The HARLEQUIN begins to play.]
[In a soft voice]
    Hurry!

[Out loud]
          Gentlemen:
you are about to see . . . .

HARLEQUIN
That he found them again
in the cool ivory.

CLOWN
You are about to see . . . . *[Exits]*

HARLEQUIN
[Exiting]
    The great turning wheel
of the wind and the sea.

[Sound of the hunting horns. Enter the TYPIST, wearing a tennis dress, a brightly colored beret and over the dress, a long cape made of a single layer of gauze. The FIRST MASK accompanies her. The MASK has a wild yellow dress, circa 1900, with a long train;

*amarilla cayendo como un manto y máscara blanca de yeso con
guantes hasta el codo del mismo color. Lleva sombrero amarillo y
todo el pecho de tetas altas ha de estar[32] sembrado de lentejuelas de
oro. El efecto de este personaje debe ser el de una llamarada, sobre
el fondo de azules lunares y troncos nocturnos. Habla con un leve
acento italiano.]*

MASCARA

[Riendo] ¡Un verdadero encanto!

MECANOGRAFA

Yo me fuí de su casa. Recuerdo que la tarde de mi partida había
una gran tormenta de verano y había muerto el niño de la portera.[33]
Yo crucé la biblioteca[34] y él me dijo: "¿Me habías llamado?", a lo
que yo contesté cerrando los ojos: "No". Y luego ya en la puerta
dijo: "¿Me necesitas?", y yo le dije: "No. No te necesito."

MASCARA

¡Precioso!

MECANOGRAFA

Esperaba siempre de pie[35] toda la noche hasta que yo me asomaba
a la ventana.

MASCARA

¿Y usted, señorina[36] mecanógrafa? . . .

MECANOGRAFA

No me asomaba. Pero . . . lo veía por las rendijas . . . quieto, *[saca un
pañuelo]* ¡con unos ojos! Entraba el aire como un cuchillo pero yo
no le podía hablar . . .

MASCARA

¿Per qué señorina?[37]

MECANOGRAFA

Porque me amaba demasiado.

*hair of yellow silk that falls like a mantle; and a plaster-white mask
with gloves of the same color that reach to her elbows. She wears a
yellow hat, and her whole high-breasted chest is covered with golden
spangles. This character should give the effect of a sudden flame,
against a background of lunar blue and the night tree trunks. She
speaks with a vaguely Italian accent.]*

MASK

[Laughing] Truly enchanting!

TYPIST

I had to leave his house. I remember, there was a great summer
storm the day of my departure, and the concierge's boy had just
died. I passed through the library, and he said, "You called me?"
"No," I replied, closing my eyes. And then, just when I'd reached
the door, he said, "You need me?" "No," I said. "I don't need you."

MASK

Precious!

TYPIST

He would always wait up the whole night until I appeared at the
window.

MASK

And you, signorina typist?

TYPIST

I wouldn't. But . . . I watched him through the cracks . . . so still . . . ,
[Takes out a handkerchief] with such eyes! The wind came in like a
knife, but I couldn't speak to him . . . .

MASK

Per que, signorina?

TYPIST

Because he loved me too much.

MASCARA

¡Oh mío Dío! Era igual que el conde Arturo de Italia... ¡Oh amor!

MECANOGRAFA

¿Sí?

MASCARA

En el Foyer de la Opera de París hay unas enormes balaustradas que dan al mar. El conde Arturo, con una camelia entre los labios, venía en una pequeña barca con su niño, los dos abandonados por mí. Pero yo corría las cortinas y les arrojaba un diamante. ¡Oh! ¡Qué dolchísimo tormento, amica mía?[38] *[Llora]* El conde y su niño pasaban hambre y dormían entre las ramas con un lebrel que me había regalado un señor de Rusia.

[Enérgica y suplicante] ¿No tienes un pedacito de pan para mí? ¿No tienes un pedacito de pan para mi hijo? ¿Para el niño que el conde Arturo dejó morir en la escarcha?... *[Agitada]* Y después fuí al hospital y allí supe que el conde se había casado con una gran dama romana... Y después he pedido limosna y[39] compartido mi cama con los hombres que descargan el carbón en los muelles.

MECANOGRAFA

¿Qué dices? ¿Por qué hablas así?[40]

MASCARA

[Serenándose] Digo que el conde Arturo me amaba tanto que lloraba detrás de las cortinas con su niño, mientras que yo era como una media luna de plata entre los gemelos y las luces de gas, que brillaban bajo la cúpula de la gran Opera de París.

MECANOGRAFA

¡Delicioso! ¿Y cuándo llega el conde?

MASCARA

¿Y cuándo llega tu amico?[41]

MECANOGRAFA

Tardará. Nunca es enseguida.[42]

MASK

Oh mio Dio! Just the same as Count Arturo di Italia ... oh my love!

TYPIST

Yes?

MASK

In the foyer of the Grande Opera de Paris, there are enormous balustrades that open onto the sea. Count Arturo, a camelia between his lips, would pass with his boy in a little boat. I had abandoned them both, you see. But I simply pulled the curtains closed and tossed them a diamond. Ah! Que dolce tormento, amica mia! *[Cries]* The count and his boy went hungry and slept among the branches with a greyhound that had been given me by a Russian gentleman.

[Emphatically and pleading] Can you spare a crust of bread for me? Can you spare a crust of bread for my son? For the boy Count Arturo left to die in the frost ...? *[Disturbed]* And later I went to the hospital where I learned that the count had married a great Roman lady ... and since then I've lived by begging and by sharing my bed with the men who unload the coal at the docks.

TYPIST

What are you saying? What are you talking about?

MASK

[Calming herself] I mean, Count Arturo loved me so that he'd be crying behind the curtains with his boy, while I was like a silver halfmoon among the binoculars and the gaslights that glittered beneath the dome of the Grande Opera de Paris.

TYPIST

Delicious! And when will the count come?

MASK

And when will your amico come?

TYPIST

He'll be late. It is never right away.

MASCARA

También Arturo tardará enseguida.[43] Tiene en la mano derecha una cicatriz que le hicieron con un puñal..., por mí, desde luego. *[Mostrando su mano]* ¿No la ves? *[Señalando el cuello]* Y aquí otra, ¿la ves?

MECANOGRAFA

¡Sí!, ¿pero por qué?

MASCARA

¿Per qué? ¿Per qué?[44] ¿Qué hago yo sin heridas? ¿De quién son las heridas de mi conde?

MECANOGRAFA

Tuyas. ¡Es verdad! Hace cinco años que me está esperando, pero ¡qué hermoso es esperar, con seguridad, el momento de ser amada!

MASCARA

¡Y es securo![45]

MECANOGRAFA

¡Seguro! ¡Por eso vamos a reir! De pequeña, yo guardaba los dulces para comerlos después.

MASCARA

¡Ja,ja,ja! Sí, ¿verdad? ¡Saben mejor!

[Se oyen las trompas.]

MECANOGRAFA

[Iniciando el mutis] Si viniera mi amigo, ¡tan alto!, con todo el cabello rizado, pero rizado de un modo especial,[46] tú haces como si no lo conocieras.

MASCARA

¡Claro! ¡Amica[47] mía! *[Se recoge la cola.]*

[Aparece el JOVEN. Viste un traje niker gris con medias a cuadros azules.][48]

MASK

Arturo too will be late, right away. There's a scar on his right hand where he was cut with a dagger . . . , over me, of course. *[Holding out her hand]* See it? *[Pointing to her neck]* And another here, see it?

TYPIST

Yes! But, why . . . ?

MASK

Per que? Per que? Why shouldn't I have wounds? Whose are the wounds of my count?

TYPIST

Your own! It's true! He's been waiting five years for me, but how lovely it is to wait, certain of the moment when you will be loved.

MASK

And it's certain!

TYPIST

Certain! So let's laugh! When I was little, I saved sweets to eat them later.

MASK

Ha, ha, ha! Yes, truly? They taste better!

[Sound of the hunting horns.]

TYPIST

[Begins exit] If my friend should come . . . so tall! With his hair all curls, but a special kind of curls . . . just pretend you don't know him.

MASK

But of course! Amica mia! *[Gathers her train]*

[The YOUNG MAN appears, wearing gray nickers with blue-checked stockings.]

ARLEQUIN

[Saliendo] ¡Eh!

JOVEN

¿Qué?

ARLEQUIN

¿Dónde va?

JOVEN

A mi casa.

ARLEQUIN

[Irónico] ¿Sí?

JOVEN

¡Claro! *[Empieza a andar.]*

ARLEQUIN

¡Eh! Por ahí no puede pasar.

JOVEN

¿Han cercado el parque?[49]

ARLEQUIN

Por ahí está el circo...

JOVEN

Bueno. *[Se vuelve.]*

ARLEQUIN

Lleno de espectadores definitivamente quietos.[50] *[Suave]* ¿No quiere entrar el señor?

JOVEN

[Estremecido][51] ¡No!

HARLEQUIN

[Entering] Hey!

YOUNG MAN

Yes?

HARLEQUIN

Where do you think you're going?

YOUNG MAN

Home.

HARLEQUIN

[Ironical] Is that right?

YOUNG MAN

Of course! *[Starts walking]*

HARLEQUIN

Hey! You can't go through there.

YOUNG MAN

Is the park fenced off?

HARLEQUIN

The circus is there . . . .

YOUNG MAN

Very well. *[Turns around]*

HARLEQUIN

Full of spectators who are terribly still. *[Softly]* Wouldn't you like to go in, sir?

YOUNG MAN

[Shaken] No!!

ARLEQUIN

[Enfático] El poeta Virgilio construyó una mosca de oro y murieron todas las moscas que envenenaban el aire de Nápoles: ahí dentro, en el circo, hay oro blando, suficiente para hacer una estatua del mismo tamaño . . . que usted.[52]

JOVEN

[No queriendo oir][53] ¿Está interceptada también la calle de los chopos?

ARLEQUIN

Allí están los carros y las jaulas con las serpientes.

JOVEN

Entonces volveré atrás. *[Inicia[54] el mutis.]*

PAYASO

[Saliendo por el lado opuesto] ¿Pero dónde va? Ja,ja,ja.

ARLEQUIN

Dice que va a su casa.

PAYASO

[Dando una bofetada de circo al ARLEQUIN] ¡Toma casa!

  [El ARLEQUIN cae al suelo gritando.]

ARLEQUIN

¡Ay, que me duele, que me duele! ¡Ayy![55]

PAYASO

[Al JOVEN] ¡Venga!

JOVEN

[Irritado] ¿Pero me quiere usted decir qué broma es ésta? Yo iba a mi casa, es decir, a mi casa no; a otra casa a . . .

HARLEQUIN

[Insistent] Virgil, the poet, made a fly out of gold, and all the flies that had been poisoning the air of Naples dropped dead: over there, in the circus, there's plenty of soft gold, enough to make a statue about the size . . . of you, sir.

YOUNG MAN

[Not wanting to listen] What about Poplar Street? Is that closed too?

HARLEQUIN

The wagons are there, and the cages for the serpents.

YOUNG MAN

Then I'll go back the way I came. *[Begins exit.]*

CLOWN

[Entering from the opposite side] But where do you think you're going? Ha, ha, ha.

HARLEQUIN

He says he's going home.

CLOWN

[Giving the HARLEQUIN a circus slap] Take that, home!

[The HARLEQUIN falls to the ground shouting.]

HARLEQUIN

Oh, it's killing me, it's killing me! Ohh!

CLOWN

[To the YOUNG MAN] Come forward!

YOUNG MAN

[Irritated] Would you mind telling me what kind of joke this is? I was on my way home, I mean, not home; to someone else's house to . . . .

PAYASO

[Interrumpiendo] A buscar.

JOVEN

Sí; porque lo necesito. A buscar.

PAYASO

[Alegre] ¿A buscar? . . .⁵⁶ Da la media vuelta y lo encontrarás.

LA VOZ DE LA MECANOGRAFA

[Cantando]

¿Dónde vas amor mío,
vida mía,⁵⁷ amor mío,
con el aire en un vaso
y el mar en un vidrio?

*[El ARLEQUIN ya se ha levantado. El PAYASO le hace señas.⁵⁸
El JOVEN está vuelto de espaldas y ellos salen también sin dar la
espalda, sobre las puntas de los pies, con paso de baile y el dedo sobre
los labios.]⁵⁹*

[Las luces del teatro se encienden.]⁶⁰

JOVEN

[Asombrado]

¿Dónde vas amor mío,
vida mía, amor mío,
con el aire en un vaso
y el mar en un vidrio?

MECANOGRAFA

[Apareciendo llena de júbilo]⁶¹

¿Dónde?, ¡dónde me llaman!

JOVEN

[Abrazándola]⁶²

¡Vida mía!

CLOWN

[Interrupting] To look.

YOUNG MAN

Yes; because I need to. To look.

CLOWN

[Brightly] To look . . . ? Well, turn halfway around and you'll find it.

THE VOICE OF THE TYPIST

[Singing]

Love, where are you going,
my life, my love, my own,
with the wind in a glass
and the sea in a bowl?

[The HARLEQUIN is now standing. The CLOWN makes signs to him. The YOUNG MAN has his back to them and they exit also without turning their backs to him, on tiptoe, with dance steps and putting their fingers to their lips.]

[The stage lights go up.]

YOUNG MAN

[Astonished]

Love, where are you going,
my life, my love, my own,
with the wind in a glass
and the sea in a bowl?

TYPIST

[Appearing joyfully]

Where? Wherever I'm called!

YOUNG MAN

[Embracing her]

My life!

MECANOGRAFA

[*Abrazándolo*][63]
> Contigo.

JOVEN

Te he de llevar desnuda,
flor ajada y cuerpo limpio,
al sitio donde las sedas
están temblando de frío.
Sábanas blancas te aguardan.[64]
Vámonos pronto. Ahora mismo.
Antes que en[65] las ramas giman
ruiseñores amarillos.

MECANOGRAFA

Sí; que el sol es un milano.
Mejor: un halcón de vidrio.
No: que el sol es un gran tronco
y tú la sombra de un río.
¿Cómo, si me abrazas, di
no nacen juncos y lirios
y no destiñen tus ondas[66]
el color de mi vestido?
Amor, déjame en el monte
harta de nube y rocío[67]
para verte grande y triste
cubrir un cielo dormido.[68]

JOVEN

No hables así. ¡Niña! ¡Vamos!
No quiero tiempo perdido.
Sangre pura y calor hondo
me están llevando a otro sitio.
¡Quiero vivir!

MECANOGRAFA
> ¿Con quién?

JOVEN
> Contigo.

TYPIST

[Embracing him]

> With you alone.

YOUNG MAN

I'm to bring you with me naked,
white body and wrinkled rose,
to the place where the silk
is trembling with the cold.
White sheets wait there for you.
Come quickly now. Let's go.
Before the yellow nightingales
in the trees begin to moan.

TYPIST

Yes; for the sun is a hawk.
Or a falcon of glass, I suppose.
No: the sun is a great tree trunk
and you are a river's shadow.
But while I am in your arms, dear,
tell me, if I come with you, won't
lilies and reeds be our children and
your waves change the color of my clothes?
Love, leave me up high on the mount
filled with dew and cloud all alone,
so I can watch you, sad and great,
cloak the sleeping sky in your love.

YOUNG MAN

Don't say such things. My child! Let's go!
I won't waste my time anymore.
Pure blood and a heat way deep down
are carrying me away and I go.
I want to live!

TYPIST

> Who with?

YOUNG MAN

> With you, my own.

MECANOGRAFA

¿Qué es eso que suena muy lejos?

JOVEN

¡Amor,
el día que vuelve,
amor mío!

MECANOGRAFA

[Alegre y como en sueño]
Un ruiseñor. ¡Que cante![69]
Ruiseñor gris de la tarde,
en la rama del arce,[70]
en la lira del cable.[71]
Ruiseñor: ¡te he sentido!
¡Quiero vivir!

JOVEN

¿Con quién?

MECANOGRAFA

Con la sombra de un río.

[Angustiada y refugiándose en el pecho del JOVEN.]
¿Qué es eso que suena muy lejos?[72]

JOVEN

¡Amor,
la sangre en mi garganta,
amor mío!

MECANOGRAFA

Siempre así, siempre, siempre,[73]
despiertos o dormidos.

JOVEN

[Enérgico y con pasión][74]
Nunca así, ¡nunca!, ¡nunca!
Vámonos de este sitio.

TYPIST

What's that I hear in the distance?

YOUNG MAN

Love,
it's the day coming back,
my love, my own!

TYPIST

[Brightly and as though dreaming]

A nightingale. Oh sing!
Gray nightingale of the evening,
on the branch of the maple tree,
on the harp of the wire, swinging.
Oh nightingale, I can hear you sing!
I'll live!

YOUNG MAN

Who with?

TYPIST

With a river's shadow.

[In anguish and hiding her head in the YOUNG MAN's chest.]

What's that I hear in the distance?

YOUNG MAN

Love.
It's the blood in my throat,
my love, my own!

TYPIST

Always, always, always like that,
awake or asleep.

YOUNG MAN

[Forcefully and passionately]

No, no.
Never, never, never like that!
Come leave this place. Let's go.

MECANOGRAFA

¡Espera!

JOVEN

¡Amor no espera!

MECANOGRAFA

[Se desase del JOVEN][75]

¿Dónde vas amor mío,
vida mía, amor mío,[76]
con el aire en un vaso
y el mar en un vidrio?
[Se dirige a la escalera.]

[Las cortinas del teatrito[77] se descorren y aparece la biblioteca del primer acto reducida y con los tonos muy pálidos.[78] Aparece en la escenita[79] la MASCARA amarilla. Tiene un pañuelo de encajes en la mano y aspira sin cesar mientras llora[80] un frasco de sales.]

MASCARA 1

[A la MECANOGRAFA] Ahora mismo acabo de abandonar para siempre al conde. Se ha quedado ahí detrás con su niño. *[Baja la escalera.]* Estoy segura que se morirá. ¡Pero me quiso tanto, tanto! *[Llora.]* *[A la MECANOGRAFA]* ¿Tú no lo sabías? Su niño morirá bajo la escarcha. ¡Lo he abandonado! ¿No ves qué contenta estoy? ¿No ves cómo río? *[Llora]* Ahora me buscará por todos lados. *[En el suelo]* Voy a esconderme dentro de las zarzamoras, *[en voz alta]*[81] dentro de las zarzamoras. Hablo así porque no quiero que Arturo me sienta. *[En voz alta]* ¡No te quiero![82] ¡Ya te he dicho que no te quiero! *[Se va llorando]* ¡Tú a mí, sí! Pero yo a tí no te quiero.

[Aparecen DOS CRIADOS vestidos con libreas azules y caras palidísimas que dejan en la izquierda del escenario dos taburetes blancos. Por la escenita cruza el CRIADO del primer acto, siempre andando sobre las puntas de los pies.]

MECANOGRAFA

[Al CRIADO y subiendo la escalera de la escenita] Si viene el señor que pase. *[En la escenita]* Aunque no vendrá; hasta que deba.[83]

TYPIST

Just wait a while!

YOUNG MAN

Love does not wait!

TYPIST

[Disengaging herself from the YOUNG MAN]
Love, where are you going,
my life, my love, my own,
with the wind in a glass
and the sea in a bowl?

[Goes to the stairs.]

> *[The curtains of the small theater draw aside, and the library of the first act appears, smaller and in much paler tones. The yellow MASK appears on the small stage. She has a lace handkerchief in her hand, and she constantly sniffs at a bottle of smelling salts as she cries.]*

FIRST MASK

[To the TYPIST] Just this minute, I have abandoned the count forever. He's back there with his boy. *[Descends the stairs.]* He will certainly die. But he loved me so, he loved me so! *[Cries. To the TYPIST]* Didn't you know? His boy is going to die in the frost. I've abandoned him! Don't you see how happy I am? Don't you see how I laugh? *[Cries]* Now, he'll be looking everywhere for me. *[Throws herself on the ground]* I'd better hide in the blackberries, *[Out loud]* in the blackberries. If I talk like this, it's because I don't want Arturo to hear me. *[Out loud]* I don't love you! You know I don't love you! *[Exits crying]* Yes, you love me! But no, I don't love you!

> *[Two SERVANTS appear, dressed in blue livery with very pale faces. They place two white stools on the main stage at left. The SERVANT of the first act crosses the small stage, on tiptoe as always.]*

TYPIST

[To the SERVANT, while climbing the stairs to the small stage] If the master comes, let him in. *[On the small stage]* Although he won't come; until he ought.

[El JOVEN empieza lentamente a subir la escalerita.][84]

JOVEN

[En la escenita, apasionado] ¿Estás contenta aquí?

MECANOGRAFA

¿Has escrito las cartas?

JOVEN

Arriba se está mejor, ¡vente![85]

MECANOGRAFA

¡Te he querido tanto!

JOVEN

¡Te quiero tanto!

MECANOGRAFA

¡Te querré tanto!

JOVEN

Me parece que agonizo sin tí. ¿Dónde voy si tú me dejas? No recuerdo nada. La otra no existe pero tú sí, porque me quieres.

MECANOGRAFA

Te he querido ¡amor! Te querré siempre.

JOVEN

Ahora . . .

MECANOGRAFA

¿Por qué dices ahora?

[Aparece por el escenario grande el VIEJO. Viene vestido de azul y trae un gran pañuelo en la mano, manchado de sangre, que lleva a su pecho y a su cara. Da muestras de agitación viva y observa atentamente[86] lo que pasa en la escenita.]

[The YOUNG MAN starts slowly climbing the stairs.]

YOUNG MAN

[On the small stage, passionately] Are you happy here?

TYPIST

Have you written the letters?

YOUNG MAN

It's nicer upstairs. Come up!

TYPIST

I have loved you so much!

YOUNG MAN

I love you so much!

TYPIST

I shall love you so much!

YOUNG MAN

I think I'd die without you. Where do I go if you leave me? I remember nothing. The other one doesn't even exist for me, but you do, because you love me.

TYPIST

I have loved you, my love! I shall always love you.

YOUNG MAN

Now . . . .

TYPIST

What do you mean now?

[The OLD MAN appears on the main stage. He is dressed in blue, and he carries a large, bloodstained handkerchief in his hand. He holds it to his chest and his face. He seems greatly disturbed, and he watches intently all that happens on the small stage.]

JOVEN

Yo esperaba y moría.

MECANOGRAFA

Yo moría por esperar.

JOVEN

Pero la sangre golpea en[87] mis sienes con sus nudillos de fuego, y ahora te tengo ya aquí.

VOZ

[Fuera] ¡Mi hijo! ¡Mi hijo! ¡Mi hijo! *[Cruza la escenita el NIÑO MUERTO. Viene solo y entra por una puerta de la izquierda.]*

JOVEN

¡Sí, mi hijo! Corre por dentro de mí, como una hormiguita[88] sola dentro de una caja cerrada. *[A la MECANOGRAFA]* ¡Un poco de luz para mi hijo! ¡Por favor! ¡Es tan pequeño! ¡Aplasta las naricillas en el cristal de mi corazón y, sin embargo, no tiene aire!

MASCARA 1[89]

[Apareciendo en el escenario grande] ¡Mi hijo! *[Aquí marcándose unos pasos de can-can.]*[90]

[Salen DOS MASCARAS más que presencian la escena.]

MECANOGRAFA

[Autoritaria y seca] ¿Has escrito las cartas? No es tu hijo, soy yo. Tú esperabas y me dejaste marchar, pero siempre te creías amado. ¿Es mentira lo que digo?

JOVEN

[Impaciente] No, pero . . .

MECANOGRAFA

Yo, en cambio, sabía que tú no me querrías nunca. Y, sin embargo, yo he levantado mi amor y te he cambiado y te he visto por los rincones de mi casa. *[Apasionada]* ¡Te quiero; pero más lejos de tí! He huído tanto que necesito contemplar el mar para poder evocar[91] el temblor de tu boca.

YOUNG MAN

I waited, with hope, and I was dying.

TYPIST

I was dying to wait with hope.

YOUNG MAN

But the blood pounds on my temples with its little knuckles of fire, and now I have you here with me.

VOICE

[Off] My son! My son! *[The DEAD BOY crosses the small stage, alone and entering through a door at left.]*

YOUNG MAN

Yes, my son! He runs inside of me like a little ant by itself in a closed box. *[To the TYPIST]* A bit of light for my son! Please! He's so little! He presses his nose against the glass of my heart, but he can't get any air!

FIRST MASK

[Appearing on the main stage] My son! *[Doing a few steps of the can-can]*

[Enter TWO MASKS who observe the scene.]

TYPIST

[Commanding and curt] Have you written the letters? It isn't your son, it's me. You were waiting, so you let me go, but you always thought I loved you. Do I lie?

YOUNG MAN

[Impatient] No, but . . . .

TYPIST

I, on the other hand, knew that you would never love me. And still I raised my love up, and I changed you, and I have seen you in the corners of my home. *[Passionately]* I love you; but far beyond you! I've run so far that I have to look at the sea just to recall the trembling of your lips.

VIEJO

Porque si él tiene veinte[92] años puede tener veinte lunas.

MECANOGRAFA

[Lírica] Veinte rocas,[93] veinte nortes de nieve.

JOVEN

[Irritado] Calla. Tú vendrás conmigo. Porque me quieres, y porque es necesario que yo viva.

MECANOGRAFA

Sí; te quiero pero ¡mucho más! No tienes tú ojos para verme desnuda, ni boca para besar mi cuerpo que nunca se acaba. Déjame. ¡Te quiero demasiado para poder contemplarte!

JOVEN

¡Ni un minuto más! ¡Vamos! *[La coge de las muñecas.]*

MECANOGRAFA

¡Me haces daño!, ¡amor!

JOVEN

¡Así me sientes!

MECANOGRAFA

[Dulce] Espera... Yo iré... Siempre. *[Le abraza.]*

VIEJO

Ella irá. Siéntate, amigo mío. Espera.[94]

JOVEN

[Angustiado] NO.[95]

MECANOGRAFA

[Abrazándolo][96] Estoy muy alta. ¿Por qué me dejaste? Iba a morir de frío y tuve que buscar tu amor por donde no hay gente. Pero estaré contigo. Déjame bajar poco a poco hasta tí.

OLD MAN

Sure, if he's twenty, he could be twenty moons.

TYPIST

[Lyrically] Twenty stones, twenty North Poles.

YOUNG MAN

[Irritated] Quiet. You must come with me. Because you love me, and because I need to live.

TYPIST

Yes; I love you, but much more than that! You haven't got the eyes to see me naked, or the lips to kiss my never-ending body. Let me alone. I love you too much to even look at you!

YOUNG MAN

Not a minute more! Come on! *[Takes her by the wrists]*

TYPIST

You're hurting me! My love!

YOUNG MAN

That way you'll feel me!

TYPIST

[Sweetly] Wait.... I'll come...forever. *[Embraces him]*

OLD MAN

She'll come. Sit down, my friend. Wait.

YOUNG MAN

[In anguish] NO.

TYPIST

[Embracing him] I'm still so very high up. Why did you leave me? I was about to die of the cold, and I had to look for your love where no people go. But I'll stay with you. Just let me come down to you little by little.

[Aparecen el PAYASO y el ARLEQUIN. El PAYASO trae una concertina[97] y el ARLEQUIN su violín blanco. Se sientan en los taburetes.]

PAYASO

Una música.

ARLEQUIN

De años.

PAYASO

Lunas y mares sin abrir.
¿Queda atrás?[98]

ARLEQUIN

La mortaja del aire.[99]

PAYASO

Y la música de tu violín.

[Tocan.][100]

JOVEN

[Saliendo de un sueño] ¡Vamos!

MECANOGRAFA

Sí... ¿Será posible que seas tú? ¡Así de pronto!... ¿Sin haber probado lentamente esta hermosa idea: mañana será? ¿No te da lástima de mí?

JOVEN

Arriba hay como un nido. Se oye cantar al ruiseñor... y aunque no se oiga, ¡aunque el murciélago golpee los cristales!

MECANOGRAFA

Sí, sí, pero...

JOVEN

[Enérgico] ¡Tu boca! *[La besa]*

[The CLOWN and the HARLEQUIN appear. The CLOWN has a concertina and the HARLEQUIN his white violin. They sit on the stools.]

CLOWN

Some music please.

HARLEQUIN

                Music of years.

CLOWN

Moons and seas that never opened.
What's back there?

HARLEQUIN

                The shroud of the air.

CLOWN

And the notes of your violin.

[They play.]

YOUNG MAN

[Waking from a dream] Come on!

TYPIST

Yes.... Can this possibly be you? So suddenly! Without having slowly pondered this pretty idea: wait until tomorrow? Doesn't it make you sorry for me?

YOUNG MAN

There's a kind of nest upstairs. You can hear the nightingale sing...and even if you can't, even if a bat thumps on the window!

TYPIST

Yes, yes, but....

YOUNG MAN

[Forcefully] Your lips! *[Kisses her]*

MECANOGRAFA

Más tarde . . .

JOVEN

[Apasionado] Es mejor de noche.

MECANOGRAFA

¡Yo me iré!

JOVEN

¡Sin tardar!

MECANOGRAFA

¡Yo quiero! Escucha.

JOVEN

¡Vamos!

MECANOGRAFA

Pero . . .

JOVEN

Dime.

MECANOGRAFA

¡Me iré contigo! . . .

JOVEN

¡Amor!¹⁰¹

MECANOGRAFA

[Tímida] Me iré contigo . . . ¡Así que pasen cinco años!

JOVEN

¡Ah! *[Se lleva las manos a la frente.]*¹⁰²

TYPIST

Later....

YOUNG MAN

[Passionately] It's better at night.

TYPIST

I'll come!

YOUNG MAN

Immediately!

TYPIST

I want to! Listen.

YOUNG MAN

Come on!

TYPIST

But....

YOUNG MAN

What is it.

TYPIST

I'll come with you...!

YOUNG MAN

Love!

TYPIST

[Shyly] I'll come with you... once five years pass!

YOUNG MAN

Oh! *[He brings his hands to his forehead.]*

VIEJO

[En voz baja] ¡Bravo!

[El JOVEN empieza a bajar lentamente la escalera. La MECAN-OGRAFA queda en actitud extática en el escenario. Sale el CRI-ADO de puntillas y la cubre con una gran capa blanca.]

PAYASO

Una música.

ARLEQUIN

De años.

PAYASO

Lunas y mares sin abrir.
Queda atrás[103]

ARLEQUIN

la mortaja del aire

PAYASO

Y la música de tu violín. [Tocan.]

MASCARA 1[104]

El conde besa mi retrato de amazona.

VIEJO

Vamos a no llegar, pero vamos a ir.

JOVEN

[Desesperado, al PAYASO]

La salida, ¿por dónde?

MECANOGRAFA

[En el escenario chico y como en sueños] ¡Amor! ¡Amor![105]

JOVEN

[Estremecido]

Enséñame la puerta!

OLD MAN

[In a soft voice] Bravo!

[The YOUNG MAN starts slowly descending the stairs. The TYP-IST remains on the stage in an ecstatic pose. Enter the SERVANT on tiptoe. He covers her with a large white cape.]

CLOWN

Some music please.

HARLEQUIN

Music of years.

CLOWN

Moons and seas that never opened.
What's back there . . . .

HARLEQUIN

is the shroud of the air.

CLOWN

And the notes of your violin. *[They play.]*

FIRST MASK

The count kisses the portrait of me as an amazon.

OLD MAN

We'll not get anywhere, but we'll go on.

YOUNG MAN

[Desperately to the CLOWN]
The exit, where is it?

TYPIST

[On the small stage and as though dreaming] My love! My love!

YOUNG MAN

[Shaking]
The door!

PAYASO

[Irónico, señalando a la izquierda] ¡Por allí!

ARLEQUIN

[Irónico, señalando a la derecha] ¡Por allí![106]

MECANOGRAFA

¡Te espero amor, te espero, vuelve pronto![107]

JOVEN

[Al PAYASO]

Te romperé las jaulas y las telas.
Yo sé saltar el muro.

VIEJO

[Con angustia]

Por aquí.

JOVEN

¡Quiero volver! Dejadme.

ARLEQUIN

¡Queda el viento!

PAYASO

¡Y la música de tu violín!

Telón

Acto Tercero
Cuadro Ultimo[1]

La misma biblioteca que en el primer acto.[2] A la izquierda el traje de novia puesto en un maniquí sin cabeza y sin manos. Varias maletas abiertas. A la derecha una mesa. Sale el CRIADO y la CRIADA.

CLOWN

[Ironical, pointing to left] That direction!

HARLEQUIN

[Ironical, pointing to right] That direction!

TYPIST

I'm waiting, love, I'm waiting, come back soon!

YOUNG MAN

[To the CLOWN]

I'll knock over all your cages and your tents.
I can jump a wall.

OLD MAN

[In anguish]

It's this direction.

YOUNG MAN

I want to go back! Let me go.

HARLEQUIN

The wind remains!

CLOWN

And the notes of your violin!

Curtain

Act Three
Final Scene

The same library as in the first act. At left, the wedding dress on a mannequin without head or arms. A number of open suitcases. At right, a table. Enter the SERVANT and the MAID.

CRIADA

[Asombrada] ¿Sí?

CRIADO

Ahora está de portera, pero antes fué una gran señora. Vivió[3] mucho tiempo con un conde italiano riquísimo, padre del niño que acaban de enterrar.

CRIADA

¡Pobrecito mío! ¡Qué precioso iba!

CRIADO

De esta época le viene su manía de grandeza. Por eso ha gastado todo lo que tenía en la ropa del niño y en la caja.

CRIADA

¡Y en las flores! Yo le he regalado un ramito de rosas, pero eran tan pequeñas que no las han entrado siquiera en la habitación.

JOVEN

[Entrando] Juan.

CRIADO

Señor.

[La CRIADA sale][4]

JOVEN

Dame un vaso de agua fría. *[El JOVEN da muestras de una gran desesperanza y un desfallecimiento físico.]*[5]

[El CRIADO lo sirve.]

JOVEN

¿No era ese ventanal mucho más grande?

CRIADO

No.

MAID

[Astonished] Really?

SERVANT

She may be a concierge now, but she was once a great lady. She lived for a long time with an extremely rich Italian count, the father of the boy they just buried.

MAID

Poor little boy! He looked so lovely!

SERVANT

It was then she acquired her delusions of grandeur. And so she spent everything she had on the boy's clothes and on his coffin.

MAID

And on the flowers! I gave her a little bunch of roses, but they were so small that they didn't even put them in his room.

YOUNG MAN

[Entering] Juan.

SERVANT

Yes sir.

[The MAID exits.]

YOUNG MAN

Bring me a glass of cold water. *[The YOUNG MAN shows evidence of great desperation and of physical weakness.]*

[The SERVANT serves him.]

YOUNG MAN

Wasn't this window very much larger?

SERVANT

No.

JOVEN

Es asombroso que sea tan estrecho.[6] Mi casa tenía un patio enorme, donde jugaba con mis caballitos. Cuando lo ví con veinte años[7] era tan pequeño que me pareció increíble que hubiera podido volar tanto por él.

CRIADO

¿Se encuentra bien el señor?

JOVEN

¿Se encuentra bien una fuente echando agua? Contesta.

CRIADO

[Sonriente][8] No sé . . .

JOVEN

¿Se encuentra bien una veleta girando como el viento quiere?

CRIADO

El señor pone unos ejemplos . . . Pero yo le preguntaría, si el señor lo permite . . . , ¿se encuentra bien el viento?

JOVEN

[Seco] Me encuentro bien.[9]

CRIADO

¿Descansó lo suficiente después del viaje?

JOVEN

[Bebe][10] Sí.

CRIADO

Lo celebro infinito. *[Inicia el mutis.]*

JOVEN

Juan: ¿está mi ropa preparada?[11]

YOUNG MAN

It's astonishing to find it so narrow. My house had a huge patio,
where I used to play with my little horses. I saw it when I was
twenty, and it was so small it seemed incredible to me that I could
have flown around in it so much.

SERVANT

Sir, are you feeling yourself?

YOUNG MAN

Does a fountain spouting water feel itself? Answer.

SERVANT

[Smiling] I don't know . . . .

YOUNG MAN

Does a weather vane that turns where the wind blows feel itself?

SERVANT

Sir, you have chosen some examples . . . but I would ask, if you'll
permit me, sir . . . does the wind feel itself?

YOUNG MAN

[Curt] I feel fine.

SERVANT

Have you rested well after your trip?

YOUNG MAN

[Drinks] Yes.

SERVANT

I'm so very glad to hear it. *[Begins exit]*

YOUNG MAN

Juan, are my clothes ready?

CRIADO

Sí, señor: está en su dormitorio.

JOVEN

¿Qué traje?

CRIADO

El frac. Lo he extendido en la cama.

JOVEN

[Irritado][12] ¡Pues quítalo! No quiero subir y encontrármelo tendido en la cama,[13] ¡tan grande!, ¡tan vacía! No sé a quién se le ocurrió comprarla. Yo tenía antes otra pequeña, ¿recuerdas?

CRIADO

Sí, señor: la de nogal tallado.

JOVEN

[Alegre][14] ¡Eso! La de nogal tallado, ¡qué bien se dormía en ella! Recuerdo que, siendo niño, ví nacer una luna enorme, detrás de la barandilla de sus pies..., ¿o fué por los hierros del balcón? No sé.[15] ¿Dónde está?

CRIADO

La regaló el señor.

JOVEN

[Pensando] ¿A quién?

CRIADO

[Serio] A su antigua mecanógrafa.

> *[El JOVEN queda pensativo. Pausa.]*[16]

JOVEN

[Indicando al CRIADO que se marche] Está bien.

> *[Sale el CRIADO.]*

SERVANT

Yes, sir; they are in your bedroom.

YOUNG MAN

Which suit?

SERVANT

Your tails. I've laid them out on the bed.

YOUNG MAN

[Irritated] Well take them off! I don't want to climb the stairs and find them lying on the bed, so big!, so empty! I don't know who took it into his head to buy that bed. I had a little one once, remember?

SERVANT

Yes, sir: of carved walnut.

YOUNG MAN

[Brightly] Exactly! Carved walnut . . . it was so good to sleep in it! I remember, when I was a boy, I saw a huge moon rise through the railings at its feet . . . or was it through the balcony rails? I don't know. Where is it?

SERVANT

You gave it away, sir.

YOUNG MAN

[Thinking] Who to?

SERVANT

[Solemnly] To that typist you once had.

[The YOUNG MAN is lost in thought. Pause.]

YOUNG MAN

[Indicating to the SERVANT that he may go] Very well.

[The SERVANT exits.]

JOVEN

[Con angustia] ¡Juan!

CRIADO

[Severo] Señor.

JOVEN

Me habrás puesto zapatos de charol...

CRIADO

Los que tienen cintas[17] de seda negra.

JOVEN

Seda negra... No...[18] Busca otros. *[Levantándose.]* ¿Y será posible que en esta casa esté siempre el aire enrarecido? Voy a cortar todas las flores del jardín, sobre todo esas malditas adelfas que saltan por los muros, y esa hierba que sale[19] sola a medianoche...

CRIADO

Dicen que con las anémonas y adormideras duele la cabeza a ciertas horas del día.

JOVEN

Eso será. *[Señalando al traje]*[20] También te llevas eso. Lo pones en la buhardilla.

CRIADO

¡Muy bien! *[Va a salir.]*

JOVEN

[Tímido] Y me dejas los zapatos de charol. Pero les cambias las cintas.

[Suena una[21] *campanilla.]*

CRIADO

[Entrando] Son los señoritos que vienen a jugar.

YOUNG MAN

[In anguish] Juan!

SERVANT

[Sternly] Sir.

YOUNG MAN

You put out my patent leather shoes?

SERVANT

The pair with black silk laces.

YOUNG MAN

Black silk ... no .... Find another pair. *[Rising]* How is it that the air in this house is always so heavy? I'll cut all the flowers in the garden, especially that damn oleander that always hops the wall, and those weeds that bloom only at midnight....

SERVANT

They say that at certain times of day one can get a headache from the windflowers and the poppies.

YOUNG MAN

That must be it. *[Pointing to the dress]* Take this, too. Put it in the garret.

SERVANT

Very well! *[About to exit]*

YOUNG MAN

[Shyly] And leave me the patent leather shoes. But change the laces.

[The doorbell rings.]

SERVANT

[Entering] The young gentlemen are here to play.

JOVEN

[Con fastidio] Abre.[22]

CRIADO

[En la puerta] El señor tendrá necesidad de vestirse.

JOVEN

[Saliendo] Sí. *[Sale casi como una sombra.]*

> *[Entran los JUGADORES. Son tres. Vienen de frac. Traen capas largas[23] de raso blanco que les llegan a los pies.]*

JUGADOR 1

Fué en Venecia. Un mal año de juego. Pero aquel muchacho jugaba de verdad. Estaba pálido, tan pálido que en la última jugada ya no tenía más remedio que echar el "as de coeur". Un corazón suyo, lleno de sangre. Lo echó y al ir a cogerlo *[bajando la voz]* para... *[mira a los lados]*, tenía un as de copas rebosando por los bordes y huyó bebiendo en él, con dos chicas, por el gran Canal.

JUGADOR 2

No hay que fiarse de la gente pálida, o de la gente que tiene hastío; juegan pero reservan.

JUGADOR 3

Yo jugué en la India con un viejo que, cuando ya no tenía una gota de sangre sobre las cartas y yo esperaba el momento de lanzarme sobre él, tiñó de rojo con una anilina especial todas las copas y pudo escapar entre los árboles.

JUGADOR 1[24]

Jugamos y ganamos; pero ¡qué trabajo nos cuesta! Las cartas beben rica sangre en las manos y es difícil cortar el hilo que las une.

JUGADOR 2

Pero creo que con éste... no nos equivocamos.

YOUNG MAN

[Testily] Let them in.

SERVANT

[At the door] You must dress, sir.

YOUNG MAN

[Exiting] Yes. *[Exits almost like a shadow]*

> *[Enter the CARDPLAYERS. There are three of them, wearing tails. They have long capes of white satin that reach to their feet.]*

FIRST CARDPLAYER

In Venice, it was. A bad year for the game. But that kid could really play. He was very pale, so pale that, come the last hand, he had no choice but to play his ace of hearts. A heart of his own, full of blood. He played it, but when I went to take it *[Lowering his voice]* to ... *[Looks all around him]*, why he had an ace of cups overflowing at the brim, and he ran off sipping at it, with two girls, along the Grand Canal.

SECOND CARDPLAYER

You just can't trust pale people, or people who're tired of it all. They play, but they hold back.

THIRD CARDPLAYER

I played one time in India with an old man. When there wasn't a drop of blood left on the cards and I was just waiting for the moment to jump him, he stained all the cups red with a special dye and got away through the trees.

FIRST CARDPLAYER

We go on playing, and we go on winning; but what a job it is! The cards drink thick blood from their hands, and it's hard to cut the thread that joins them.

SECOND CARDPLAYER

Still, I think with this one ... we are not mistaken.

JUGADOR 3

No sé.

JUGADOR 1

[Al 2] No aprenderás nunca a conocer a tus clientes. ¿A éste? La vida se le escapa en dos chorros[25] por sus pupilas, que mojan la comisura de sus labios y le tiñen de coral[26] la pechera del frac.

JUGADOR 2

Sí. Pero acuérdate del niño que en Suecia jugó con nosotros, casi agonizante, y por poco sí nos deja ciegos a los tres con el chorro de sangre que nos echó.

JUGADOR 3

¡La baraja![27] *[Saca una baraja]*

JUGADOR 2

Hay que estar muy suaves con él, para que no reaccione.

JUGADOR 1[28]

Y aunque ni a la *otra*[29] ni a la señorita mecanógrafa se les ocurrirá venir por aquí hasta que pasen cinco años, si es que vienen...

JUGADOR 3[30]

[Riendo] ¡Si es que vienen! Ja, ja, ja.

JUGADOR 1

[Riendo][31] No estará mal ser rápidos en la jugada.

JUGADOR 2

El guarda un as.

JUGADOR 3

Un corazón joven, donde es probable que resbalen las flechas.

JUGADOR 1

[Alegre y profundo] ¡Cá! Yo compré[32] unas flechas en un tiro al blanco...

THIRD CARDPLAYER

I don't know.

FIRST CARDPLAYER

[To SECOND] Will you never learn to know your customers! This one? Life pours out of his pupils in two floods, wetting the line between his lips and staining his white shirt the color of coral.

SECOND CARDPLAYER

Yes, but remember the boy in Sweden who was nearly dead when he played us. And the spurt of blood he sprayed all over us was practically enough to blind us.

THIRD CARDPLAYER

The deck! *[Takes out a deck of cards]*

SECOND CARDPLAYER

We've got to go very easy with him, so we don't scare him off.

FIRST CARDPLAYER

And though I doubt either the other woman or the lady typist will take it into her head to show up around here until five years pass, if they ever do . . . .

THIRD CARDPLAYER

[Laughing] If they ever do! Ha, ha, ha.

FIRST CARDPLAYER

[Laughing] It wouldn't be a bad idea to play him fast.

SECOND CARDPLAYER

He's holding an ace.

THIRD CARDPLAYER

A young heart. Arrows will probably slide right off it.

FIRST CARDPLAYER

[Brightly and wisely] Naa! I bought some arrows at a target shoot . . . .

JUGADOR 3[33]

[Con curiosidad] ¿Dónde?

JUGADOR 1

[Con broma][34] En un tiro al blanco, que no sólamente se clavan[35] sobre el acero más duro sino sobre la gasa más fina, ¡y ésto sí que es difícil! *[Ríen.]*

JUGADOR 2

[Riendo][36] ¡En fin! ¡Ya veremos!

[Aparece el JOVEN vestido de frac.]

JOVEN

¡Señores! *[Les da la mano.]* Han venido muy temprano. Hace demasiado calor.

JUGADOR 1

¡No tanto!

JUGADOR 2

[Al JOVEN] ¡Elegante como siempre![37]

JUGADOR 1

Tan elegante que ya no debía desnudarse más, nunca.[38]

JUGADOR 3

Hay veces[39] que la ropa nos cae tan bien, que ya no quisiéramos...

JUGADOR 2

[Interrumpiendo] Que ya no podemos arrancarla del cuerpo.

JOVEN

[Con fastidio] ¡Demasiado amables!

[Aparece el CRIADO con una bandeja y copas que deja en la mesa.]

JOVEN

¿Comenzamos?

THIRD CARDPLAYER

[Curiously] Where?

FIRST CARDPLAYER

[Joking] At a target shoot. They stick as well to the hardest steel as to the finest gauze, and that is really difficult! *[They laugh.]*

SECOND CARDPLAYER

[Laughing] Well, well! We shall see!

> *[The YOUNG MAN appears, dressed in tails.]*

YOUNG MAN

Gentlemen! *[Shakes their hands]* You're here early. It's awfully hot.

FIRST CARDPLAYER

Not too!

SECOND CARDPLAYER

[To the YOUNG MAN] Elegant as always!

FIRST CARDPLAYER

So elegant you shouldn't undress again ever.

THIRD CARDPLAYER

Sometimes clothes fit us so well, we wish . . . .

SECOND CARDPLAYER

[Interrupting] We just can't tear them from our body.

YOUNG MAN

[Testily] You're too kind!

> *[The SERVANT appears with a tray full of cups that he leaves on the table.]*

YOUNG MAN

Shall we begin?

[Se sientan los tres.]

JUGADOR 1

Dispuestos.

JUGADOR 2

[En voz baja] ¡Buen ojo!

JUGADOR 3

¿No se sienta?

JOVEN

No . . . , prefiero jugar de pie.

JUGADOR 1[40]

¿De pie?

JUGADOR 2

[Bajo] Tendrás necesidad de ahondar mucho.

JUGADOR 1

[Repartiendo cartas] ¿Cuántas?

JOVEN

Cuatro. *[Se las da y a los demás.]*[41]

JUGADOR 3

[Bajo] Jugada nula.

JOVEN

¡Qué cartas más frías! Nada. *[Las deja sobre la mesa.]* ¿Y ustedes? . . .

JUGADOR 1

[Con voz grave][42] Nada. *[Le da cartas otra vez.]*

[The three sit down.]

FIRST CARDPLAYER

Ready.

SECOND CARDPLAYER

[In a soft voice] Look sharp!

THIRD CARDPLAYER

Won't you sit down?

YOUNG MAN

No . . . , I'd rather play standing up.

FIRST CARDPLAYER

Standing up?

SECOND CARDPLAYER

[Softly] You'll have to get it very deep.

FIRST CARDPLAYER

[Dealing cards] How many?

YOUNG MAN

Four. *[Deals to him and to the others]*

THIRD CARDPLAYER

[Softly] No play.

YOUNG MAN

What cold cards! Nothing. *[Leaves them on the table]* You all . . . ?

FIRST CARDPLAYER

[In a serious voice] Nothing. *[Deals the cards again.]*

JUGADOR 2

Nada.[43] *[Mirando sus cartas]* ¡Magnífico!

JUGADOR 3

Nada.[44] *[Mirando sus cartas y con inquietud]* ¡Vamos a ver!

JUGADOR 1

[Al JOVEN] Usted juega.

JOVEN

[Alegre] ¡Y juego![45] *[Echa una carta sobre la mesa.]*

JUGADOR 1

[Enérgico] ¡Y yo!

JUGADOR 2

¡Y yo!

JUGADOR 3

¡Y yo!

JOVEN

[Excitado, con una carta][46] ¿Y ahora? . . .

> *[Los tres JUGADORES enseñan tres[47] cartas. El JOVEN se detiene y se la[48] oculta en la mano.]*

JOVEN

Juan. Sirve licor a estos señores.

JUGADOR 1

[Suave] ¿Tiene usted la bondad de la carta?

JOVEN

[Angustiado] ¿Qué licor desean?

JUGADOR 2

[Dulce] ¿La carta? . . .

SECOND CARDPLAYER

Nothing. *[Looking at his cards]* Terrific!

THIRD CARDPLAYER

Nothing. *[Looking at his cards and nervously]* We shall see.

FIRST CARDPLAYER

[To the YOUNG MAN] Your play.

YOUNG MAN

[Brightly] Here's mine! *[Throws one card on the table]*

FIRST CARDPLAYER

[Forcefully] And mine!

SECOND CARDPLAYER

And mine!

THIRD CARDPLAYER

And mine!

YOUNG MAN

[Excited, with a card] And now . . . ?

> *[The three CARDPLAYERS play three cards. The YOUNG MAN hesitates and hides his behind his hand.]*

YOUNG MAN

Juan. Serve these gentlemen a cup of liqueur.

FIRST CARDPLAYER

[Gently] Be so kind as to play your card.

YOUNG MAN

[In anguish] What would you like to drink?

SECOND CARDPLAYER

[Sweetly] The card . . . ?

JOVEN

[Al JUGADOR 3] A usted seguramente le gustará el anís. Es una bebida . . .

JUGADOR 3

Por favor . . . , la carta . . .

JOVEN

[Al CRIADO, que entra] ¿Cómo no hay whisky?[49] *[En el momento que el CRIADO entra los JUGADORES quedan silenciosos con las cartas en la mano]* ¿Ni coñac? . . .

JUGADOR 1

[En voz baja y ocultándose del CRIADO] ¡La carta!

JOVEN

[Angustiado] El coñac es una bebida para hombres que saben resistir.

JUGADOR 2

[Enérgico, pero en voz baja] ¡Su carta![50]

JOVEN

¿O prefieren chartreuse?

[Sale el CRIADO.]

JUGADOR 1

[Levantando y enérgico] Tenga la bondad de jugar.

JOVEN

Ahora mismo. Pero beberemos . . .

JUGADOR 3

[Fuerte] ¡Hay que jugar!

YOUNG MAN

[To the THIRD CARDPLAYER] I'll bet you like anise. It's a drink . . . .

THIRD CARDPLAYER

If you please . . . , the card . . . .

YOUNG MAN

[To the SERVANT, who enters] Why is there no whiskey?
[The moment the SERVANT enters, the CARDPLAYERS fall silent with their cards in their hands.] Or cognac . . . ?

FIRST CARDPLAYER

[In a soft voice and concealing himself from the SERVANT] The card!

YOUNG MAN

[In anguish] Now cognac is a drink for men who can fight.

SECOND CARDPLAYER

[Forcefully, but in a soft voice] Your card!

YOUNG MAN

Or would you prefer chartreuse?

[The SERVANT exits.]

FIRST CARDPLAYER

[Rising and forcefully] Be so kind as to play.

YOUNG MAN

Right now. But shall we drink . . . .

THIRD CARDPLAYER

[Powerfully] You must play!

JOVEN

[Agonizante] Sí, sí. ¡Un poco de chartreuse! El chartreuse es como una gran noche de luna verde dentro de un castillo, donde hay un joven con unas calzas[51] de oro.

JUGADOR 1

[Fuerte] Es necesario que usted nos dé su as.

JOVEN

[Aparte] ¡Mi corazón!

JUGADOR 2

[Enérgico] Porque hay que ganar o perder... Vamos. ¡Su carta!

JUGADOR 3

¡Venga!

JUGADOR 1

¡Haga juego!

JOVEN

[Con dolor] ¡Mi carta!

JUGADOR 1

¡La última!

JOVEN

¡Juego!

> *[Pone la carta sobre la mesa. En este momento en los anaqueles de la biblioteca aparece un gran[52] "as de coeur" iluminado. El JUGADOR 1 saca una pistola y dispara sin ruido con una flecha. El as[53] desaparece y el JOVEN se lleva las manos al corazón.]*

JUGADOR 1

¡Hay que vivir![54]

YOUNG MAN

[Agonizing] Yes, yes. A little chartreuse! Chartreuse is like a great night under a green moon, in a castle where there's a young man wearing golden tights.

FIRST CARDPLAYER

[Powerfully] You have to give us your ace.

YOUNG MAN

[Aside] My heart!

SECOND CARDPLAYER

Because one must either win or lose . . . . Come on. Your card!

THIRD CARDPLAYER

Let's go!

FIRST CARDPLAYER

Make your play!

YOUNG MAN

[Painfully] My card!

FIRST CARDPLAYER

The last one!

YOUNG MAN

Here it is!

[He places the card on the table. At that moment a great ace of hearts appears illuminated against the bookshelves. The FIRST CARDPLAYER draws a pistol and soundlessly fires an arrow. The ace disappears, and the YOUNG MAN's hands go to his heart.]

FIRST CARDPLAYER

One must live!

JUGADOR 2
¡No hay que esperar!

JUGADOR 3
¡Corta! Corta bien.

> *[El JUGADOR 1 con unas tijeras da unos cortes en el aire.]*

JUGADOR 1
[En voz baja] ¡Vamos!

JUGADOR 2
¡De prisa!

JUGADOR 3
¡No hay que esperar nunca! ¡Hay que vivir![55] *[Salen.]*

JOVEN
¡Juan! ¡Juan![56]

ECO
¡Juan! ¡Juan!

JOVEN
[Agonizante] Lo he perdido todo.

ECO
Lo he perdido todo.

JOVEN
Mi amor . . .

ECO
Amor.[57]

SECOND CARDPLAYER

One mustn't wait!

THIRD CARDPLAYER

Cut! Cut carefully.

[The FIRST CARDPLAYER makes a few cuts in the air with a pair of scissors.]

FIRST CARDPLAYER

[In a soft voice] Come on!

SECOND CARDPLAYER

Quickly!

THIRD CARDPLAYER

One must never wait! One must live! *[They exit.]*

YOUNG MAN

Juan! Juan!

ECHO

Juan! Juan!

YOUNG MAN

[Agonizing] I have lost everything.

ECHO

I have lost everything .

YOUNG MAN

My love. . .

ECHO

Love.

JOVEN

Juan.

[El JOVEN muere en el sofá.][58]

ECO

Juan.[59]

[Aparece el CRIADO con un candelabro encendido. El reloj da las doce.]

Telón

Granada 19 de Agosto 1931[60]
Huerta de San Vicente

YOUNG MAN

Juan.

[The YOUNG MAN dies on the sofa.]

ECHO

Juan.

[The SERVANT appears with a lighted candelabra. The clock strikes twelve.]

Curtain

Granada, August 19, 1931
Huerta de San Vicente

Arlequín veneciano [1927]

Venetian Harlequin

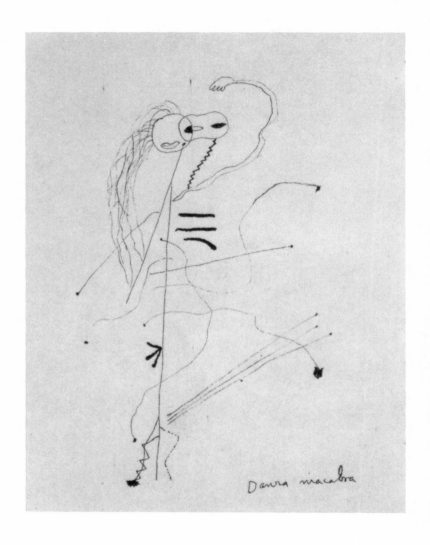

Danza macabra [h. 1927-1928]

Danse Macabre

El Paseo de Buster Keaton
Buster Keaton's Outing

El Paseo de Buster Keaton

Personajes

BUSTER KEATON	EL GALLO
EL BUHO	UN NEGRO
UNA AMERICANA	UNA JOVEN

GALLO

Kikirikí.

> *[Sale BUSTER KEATON con sus cuatro hijos de la mano.]*

BUSTER KEATON

[Saca un puñal de madera y los mata.] Pobres hijitos míos.

GALLO

Kikirikí.

BUSTER KEATON

[Contando los cuerpos en tierra.] Uno, dos, tres y cuatro.

> *[Coge una bicicleta y se va.]*

> *[Entre las viejas llantas de goma y bidones de gasolina, un NEGRO come su sombrero de paja.]*

BUSTER KEATON

¡Qué hermosa tarde!

> *[Un loro revolotea en el cielo neutro.]*

Buster Keaton's Outing

Characters

BUSTER KEATON	THE ROOSTER
THE OWL	A BLACK MAN
AN AMERICAN LADY	A YOUNG WOMAN

ROOSTER

Cockadoodledoo.

> *[Enter BUSTER KEATON leading his four children by the hand.]*

BUSTER KEATON

[Draws a wooden knife and kills them.] My poor little children.

ROOSTER

Cockadoodledoo.

BUSTER KEATON

[Counting the bodies on the ground.] One, two, three, four.

> *[Mounts a bicycle and rides off.]*

> *[Among the old rubber tires and the gasoline drums, A BLACK MAN eats his straw hat.]*

BUSTER KEATON

What a lovely afternoon!

> *[A parrot circles in the colorless sky.]*

BUSTER KEATON

Da gusto pasearse en bicicleta.

EL BUHO

Chirri, chirri, chirri, chi.

BUSTER KEATON

¡Qué bien cantan los pajarillos!

EL BUHO

Chirrrrrrrrrrrr.

BUSTER KEATON

Es emocionante.

> *[Pausa. BUSTER KEATON cruza inefable los juncos y el campillo de centeno. El paisaje se achica entre las ruedas de la máquina. La bicicleta tiene una sola dimensión. Puede entrar en los libros y tenderse en el horno del pan. La bicicleta de BUSTER KEATON no tiene el sillín de caramelo y los pedales de azúcar, como quisieran los hombres malos. Es una bicicleta como todas, pero la única empapada de inocencia. Adán y Eva correrían asustados si vieran un vaso lleno de agua, y acariciarían, en cambio, la bicicleta de KEATON.]*

BUSTER KEATON

¡Ay amor, amor!

> *[BUSTER KEATON cae al suelo. La bicicleta se le escapa. Corre detrás de dos grandes mariposas grises. Va como loco, a medio milímetro del suelo.]*

BUSTER KEATON

[Levantándose.] No quiero decir nada. ¿Qué voy a decir?

UNA VOZ

Tonto.

BUSTER KEATON

It's fun to ride a bike.

THE OWL

Whoo, whoo, whoo, who.

BUSTER KEATON

How sweetly the little birds are singing!

THE OWL

Whooooooo.

BUSTER KEATON

What a thrill.

> [*Pause. BUSTER KEATON rides indescribably along past the bulrushes and the little field of rye. The landscape shrinks between the wheels of the machine. The bicycle has only one dimension. It can fit inside books and lie flat in the bread oven. BUSTER KEATON's bicycle does not have a caramel seat and pedals of sugar, as evil men might wish. It is a bicycle like any other, except that it is the only one steeped in innocence. Adam and Eve would recoil in fright if they saw a glass of water; on the other hand, they would caress KEATON's bike.*]

BUSTER KEATON

Love, oh love!

> [*BUSTER KEATON falls to the ground. The bicycle gets away. It zooms behind two big gray butterflies. It runs like crazy, half-an-inch off the ground.*]

BUSTER KEATON

[*Rising.*] I have nothing to say. What can I say?

A VOICE

Stupid.

BUSTER KEATON

Bueno.[1]

[Sigue andando. Sus ojos, infinitos y tristes, como los de una bestia recién nacida, sueñan lirios, ángeles y cinturones de seda. Sus ojos, que son de culo de vaso. Sus ojos de niño tonto. Que son feísimos. Que son bellísimos. Sus ojos de avestruz. Sus ojos humanos en el equilibrio seguro de la melancolía. A lo lejos se ve Filadelfia. Los habitantes de esta urbe ya saben que el viejo poema de la maquina Singer puede circular entre las grandes rosas de los invernaderos, aunque no podrán comprender nunca qué sutilísima diferencia poética existe entre una taza de té caliente y otra taza de té frío. A lo lejos brilla Filadelfia.]

BUSTER KEATON

Esto es un jardín.

[Una AMERICANA con los ojos de celuloide viene por la hierba.][2]

AMERICANA

Buenas tardes.

[BUSTER KEATON sonríe y mira en "gros plan" los zapatos de la dama. ¡Oh, qué zapatos! No debemos admitir esos zapatos. Se necesitan las pieles de tres cocodrilos para hacerlos.]

BUSTER KEATON

Yo quisiera . . .

AMERICANA

¿Tiene usted una espada adornada con hojas de mirto?

[BUSTER KEATON se encoge de hombros y levanta el pie derecho.]

AMERICANA

¿Tiene usted un anillo con la piedra envenenada?

[BUSTER KEATON cierra lentamente los ojos y levanta el pie izquierdo.]

AMERICANA

¿Pues entonces?

BUSTER KEATON

O.K.

[Continuing, on foot. His eyes, infinite and sad, like those of a newborn animal, dream irises, angels and silken belts. His eyes, which are of rhinestones. His eyes of a stupid boy. Which are so ugly. Which are so beautiful. His eyes of an ostrich. His human eyes in the steady equilibrium of sadness. Philadelphia can be seen in the distance. The inhabitants of that city already know that the old poem of the Singer sewing machine can go back and forth between the great roses of the conservatories, although they will never understand the very subtle poetic difference there is between a cup of hot tea and another cup of cold tea. Philadelphia glows in the distance.]

BUSTER KEATON

Here is a garden.

[An AMERICAN LADY with celluloid eyes comes through the grass.]

AMERICAN LADY

Good afternoon.

[BUSTER KEATON smiles and looks rudely at the lady's shoes. Oh, what shoes! We should not permit such shoes. In order to make them, the skin of three crocodiles was required.]

BUSTER KEATON

I wish . . . .

AMERICAN LADY

Have you got a sword etched with myrtle leaves?

[BUSTER KEATON shrugs and lifts his right foot.]

AMERICAN LADY

Have you got a ring with the poison stone?

[BUSTER KEATON slowly closes his eyes and lifts his left foot.]

AMERICAN LADY

Well then?

[Cuatro serafines con las alas de gasa celeste bailan entre las flores. Las señoritas de la ciudad tocan el piano como si montaran en bicicleta. El vals, la luna y las canoas estremecen el precioso corazón de nuestro amigo. Con gran sorpresa de todos, el Otoño ha invadido el jardín, como el agua al geométrico terrón de azúcar.]

BUSTER KEATON

[Suspirando.] Quisiera ser un cisne. Pero no puedo aunque quisiera. Porque ¿dónde dejaría mi sombrero? ¿Dónde mi cuello de pajarita y mi corbata de moaré? ¡Qué desgracia!

[Una JOVEN, cintura de avispa y alto cuculé, viene montada en bicicleta. Tiene cabeza de ruiseñor.]

JOVEN

¿A quién tengo el honor de saludar?

BUSTER KEATON

[Con una reverencia.] A Buster Keaton.

[La JOVEN se desmaya y cae de la bicicleta. Sus piernas a listas tiemblan en el césped como dos cebras agonizantes. Un gramófono decía en mil espectáculos a la vez: "En América hay ruiseñores."]

BUSTER KEATON

[Arrodillándose.] Señorita Eleonora, ¡perdóneme, que yo no he sido! ¡Señorita! *[Bajo.]* ¡Señorita! *[Más bajo.]* ¡Señorita! *[La besa.]*

[En el horizonte de Filadelfia luce la estrella rutilante de los policías.]

Fin

[Four seraphim with wings of sky blue gauze dance among the flowers. The young ladies of the city play the piano as though riding a bicycle. The waltz, the moon and the motorboats shake the precious heart of our friend. To the great surprise of everyone, autumn has invaded the garden, like water in a geometrical sugar lump.]

BUSTER KEATON

[Sighing] I wish I were a swan. But I can't be no matter how I wish. Because, where would I leave my hat? Where my wing collar and my moire tie? What misfortune!

[A YOUNG WOMAN, wasp-waisted and with a high topknot, passes riding a bicycle. She has the head of a nightingale.]

YOUNG WOMAN

Whom do I have the honor of addressing?

BUSTER KEATON

[With a bow.] Buster Keaton.

[The YOUNG WOMAN faints and falls from her bicycle. Her striped legs tremble on the grass like two dying zebras. A gramophone played in a thousand shows at once: "There are nightingales in America."]

BUSTER KEATON

[Kneeling down.] Miss Eleanor, forgive me, it wasn't my fault! Miss! *[Softly.]* Miss! *[More softly.]* Miss! *[He kisses her.]*

[On the horizon of Philadelphia shines the twinkling star of the police.]

End

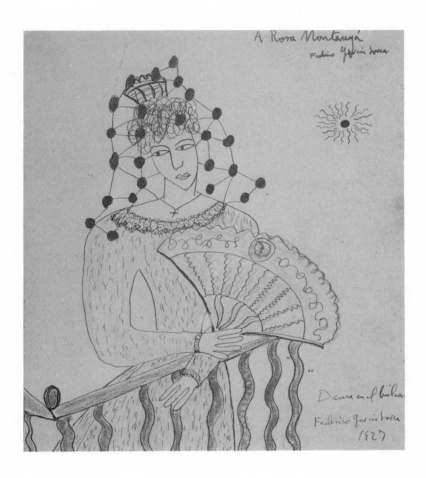

Dama en el balcón [1927]

Lady on the Balcony

Sueño del marino [1927]

Dream of the Sailor

La Doncella, el Marinero y el Estudiante

The Maiden, the Sailor and the Student

La Doncella, el Marinero y el Estudiante

Personajes

LA DONCELLA	EL ESTUDIANTE
EL MARINERO	LA MADRE
UNA VIEJA	

BALCON

VIEJA

[*En la calle.*) ¡Caracoleeees! Se guisan con hierbabuena, azafrán y hojas de laurel.

DONCELLA

Caracolitos del campo. Parecen amontonados en la cesta una antigua ciudad de la China.

VIEJA

Esta vieja los vende. Son grandes y oscuros. Cuatro de ellos pueden con una culebra. ¡Qué caracoles! Dios mío, ¡qué caracoles!

DONCELLA

Déjeme que borde. Mis almohadas no tienen iniciales y esto me da mucho miedo... Porque, ¿qué muchachilla en el mundo no tiene marcada su ropa?

VIEJA

¿Cómo es tu gracia?

The Maiden, the Sailor and the Student

Characters

THE MAIDEN   **THE STUDENT**
THE SAILOR   **THE MOTHER**
AN OLD WOMAN

BALCONY

OLD WOMAN

[On the street.] Snaiiiils! Cook them in saffron, mint and laurel leaves.

MAIDEN

Little snails from the country. They look like an old Chinese city all jumbled up in the basket.

OLD WOMAN

This old woman is selling them. They are big and dark. Four of them could kill a snake. Such snails! My God, such snails!

MAIDEN

Leave me to my embroidery. My pillows have no monograms and it makes me so afraid . . . . Why, what girl in all the world hasn't marked her clothes?

OLD WOMAN

What are your initials?

DONCELLA

Yo bordo en mis ropas todo el alfabeto.

VIEJA

¿Para qué?

DONCELLA

Para que el hombre que esté conmigo me llame de la manera que guste.

VIEJA

[*Triste.*] Entonces eres una sinvergüenza.

DONCELLA

[*Bajando los ojos.*] Sí.

VIEJA

¿Te llamarás María, Rosa, Trinidad? ¿Segismunda?

DONCELLA

Y más, y más.

VIEJA

¿Eustaquia? ¿Dorotea? ¿Jenara?

DONCELLA

Y más, más, más . . .

[*La DONCELLA eleva las palmas de sus manos palidecidas por el insomnio de la seda y los marcadores. La VIEJA huye, arrimada a la pared, hacia su Siberia de trapos oscuros, donde agoniza la cesta llena de mendrugos de pan.*]

DONCELLA

A, B, C, D, E, F, G, H, I, J, K, L, M, N. Ya está bien. Voy a cerrar el balcón. Detrás de los cristales seguiré bordando.

[*Pausa.*]

MAIDEN

I stitch the entire alphabet onto my clothes.

OLD WOMAN

What for?

MAIDEN

So the man who is with me can call me anything he likes.

OLD WOMAN

[Sad.] Then you're a shameless hussy.

MAIDEN

[Lowering her eyes.] Yes.

OLD WOMAN

You'll answer to Maria, Rosa, Trinidad? Segismunda?

MAIDEN

And more, and more.

OLD WOMAN

Eustaquia? Dorotea? Jenara?

MAIDEN

And more, more, more . . . .

[The MAIDEN lifts up the palms of her hands, pale from the sleeplessness of the silk and the samplers. The OLD WOMAN runs away, hugging tight to the wall, towards her Siberia of dark rags, where the basket full of breadcrusts is dying.]

MAIDEN

A, B, C, D, E, F, G, H, I, J, K, L, M, N. That's better. I'll shut the balcony and then keep on stitching behind the windows.

[Pause.]

LA MADRE

[Dentro.] Hija, hija, ¿estás llorando?

DONCELLA

No. Es que empieza a llover.

[Una canoa automóvil llena de banderas azules[1] cruza la bahía, dejando atrás su canto tartamudo. La lluvia pone a la ciudad un birrete de doctor en Letras. En las tabernas del puerto comienza el gran carrusel de los marineros borrachos.]

DONCELLA

[Cantando.]
> A, B, C, D.
> ¿Con qué letra me quedaré?
> Marinero empieza con M,
> y Estudiante empieza con E,
> A, B, C, D.

MARINERO

[Entrando.] Yo.

DONCELLA

Tú.

MARINERO

[Triste.] Poca cosa es un barco.

DONCELLA

Le pondré banderas y dulces.

MARINERO

Si el capitán quiere.

[Pausa.]

DONCELLA

[Afligida.] ¡Poca cosa es un barco!

THE MOTHER

[Off.] Daughter, daughter, are you crying?

MAIDEN

No. It's starting to rain.

> *[A motorboat full of blue flags crosses the bay, leaving a stuttering song in its wake.*
> *The rain crowns the city in the splendid cap of a doctor-in-letters.*
> *In the bars near the port, drunken sailors begin to spin like merry-go-rounds.]*

MAIDEN

[Singing.]

> A, B, C, D.
> Which is the letter for me?
> Sailor begins with S-A,
> student begins with S-T,
> A, B, C, D.

SAILOR

[Entering.] Me.

MAIDEN

You.

SAILOR

[Sad.] A boat isn't much to offer.

MAIDEN

I'll deck it with flags and sweets.

SAILOR

If the captain agrees.

> *[Pause.]*

MAIDEN

[Sorrowful.] A boat's a little thing!

MARINERO

Lo llenaré de puntillas bordadas.

DONCELLA

Si mi madre me deja.

MARINERO

Ponte de pie.

DONCELLA

¿Para qué?

MARINERO

Para verte.

DONCELLA

[Se levanta.] Ya estoy.

MARINERO

¡Qué hermosos muslos tienes!

DONCELLA

De niña monté en bicicleta.

MARINERO

Yo en un delfín.

DONCELLA

También eres hermoso.

MARINERO

Cuando estoy desnudo.

DONCELLA

¿Qué sabes hacer?

SAILOR

I'll fill it with embroidered lace.

MAIDEN

If my mother lets me.

SAILOR

Stand up.

MAIDEN

What for?

SAILOR

So I can see you.

MAIDEN

[Getting up.] Here I am.

SAILOR

What handsome thighs you have!

MAIDEN

When I was little, I rode a bicycle.

SAILOR

And I, a dolphin.

MAIDEN

You're handsome too.

SAILOR

When I'm naked.

MAIDEN

What do you know how to do?

MARINERO

Remar.

[El MARINERO toca el acordeón polvoriento y cansado como un siglo XVII.]

ESTUDIANTE

[Entrando.] Va demasiado de prisa.

DONCELLA

¿Quién va de prisa?

ESTUDIANTE

El siglo.

DONCELLA

Estás azorado.

ESTUDIANTE

Es que huyo.

DONCELLA

¿De quién?

ESTUDIANTE

Del año que viene.

DONCELLA

¿No has visto mi cara?

ESTUDIANTE

Por eso me paro.

DONCELLA

No eres moreno.

ESTUDIANTE

Es que vivo de noche.

SAILOR

To stroke.

[The SAILOR plays an accordion dusty and tired like a 17th Century.]

STUDENT

[Entering] It's going too fast.

MAIDEN

Who's going too fast?

STUDENT

The century.

MAIDEN

You're all mixed up.

STUDENT

Because I'm running.

MAIDEN

Running from what?

STUDENT

From the coming year.

MAIDEN

Haven't you seen my face?

STUDENT

That's why I stopped.

MAIDEN

You haven't got a tan.

STUDENT

Because I live at night.

DONCELLA

¿Qué quieres?

ESTUDIANTE

Dáme agua.

DONCELLA

No tenemos aljibe.

ESTUDIANTE

¡Pues yo me muero de sed!

DONCELLA

Te daré leche de mis senos.

ESTUDIANTE

[Encendido.] Endulza mi boca.

DONCELLA

Pero soy doncella.

ESTUDIANTE

Si me echas una escala, viviré esta noche contigo.

DONCELLA

Eres blanco y estarás muy frío.

ESTUDIANTE

Tengo mucha fuerza en los brazos.

DONCELLA

Yo te dejaría si mi madre quisiera.

ESTUDIANTE

Anda.

MAIDEN

What do you want?

STUDENT

Give me water.

MAIDEN

We haven't got a well.

STUDENT

I'm dying of thirst!

MAIDEN

I'll give you milk from my breasts.

STUDENT

[Ardent] Sweeten my mouth.

MAIDEN

But I'm a maiden.

STUDENT

If you'll drop me a ladder, I'll spend tonight with you.

MAIDEN

You're white and you'll be very cold.

STUDENT

I have plenty of strength in my arms.

MAIDEN

I'd let you if my mother would agree.

STUDENT

Come on.

DONCELLA

No.

ESTUDIANTE

¿Y por qué no?

DONCELLA

Pues porque no . . .

ESTUDIANTE

Anda . . .

DONCELLA

No.

[Alrededor de la luna gira una rueda de bergantines oscuros. Tres sirenas chapoteando en las olas engañan a los carabineros del acantilado. La DONCELLA, en su balcón, piensa dar un salto desde la letra Z y lanzarse al abismo. EMILIO PRADOS y MANOLITO ALTOLAGUIRRE, enharinados por el miedo del mar, la quitan suavemente de la baranda.]

Fin

MAIDEN

No.

STUDENT

And why not?

MAIDEN

Well because I don't . . . .

STUDENT

Come on . . . .

MAIDEN

No.

[*A circle of dark vessels revolves around the moon. Three sirens splashing in the waves deceive the coast-guard on the cliff. The MAIDEN, on her balcony, considers jumping headlong off the letter Z and into the abyss. EMILIO PRADOS and MANOLITO ALTOLAGUIRRE, as white as flour with the fear of the sea, carry her gently away from the railing.*]

End

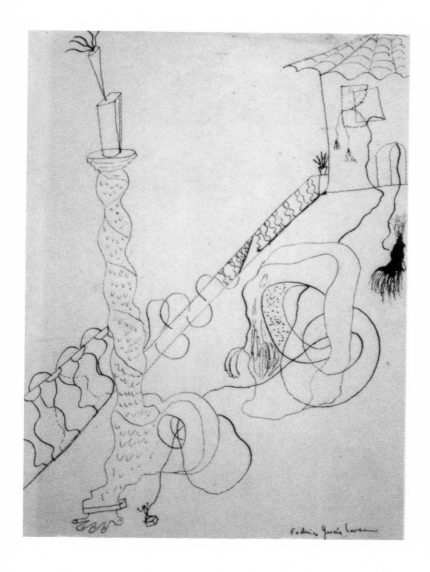

Terraza con columna [h. 1934–1936]

Terrace with Column

Muchacha con miriñaque y sortija [1924]

Girl with Hoop Skirt and Ring

Quimera
Chimera

Quimera[1]

Personajes

ENRIQUE	NIÑA
VIEJO	VOCES
MUJER	

PUERTA

ENRIQUE

Adiós.

SEIS VOCES

[Dentro.] Adiós.

ENRIQUE

Estaré mucho tiempo en la sierra.

VOZ

Una ardilla.

ENRIQUE

Sí, una ardilla para tí y además cinco pájaros que no los haya tenido antes ningún niño.

VOZ

No, yo quiero un lagarto.

VOZ

Y yo un topo.

Chimera

Characters

ENRIQUE	GIRL
OLD MAN	VOICES
WIFE	

DOOR

ENRIQUE

Goodbye.

SIX VOICES

[Off.] Goodbye.

ENRIQUE

I'll be up in the mountains for a long time.

VOICE

A squirrel.

ENRIQUE

Yes, for you a squirrel, and besides that, five birds that no child before you has ever had.

VOICE

No, I want a lizard.

VOICE

And I a mole.

ENRIQUE

Sois muy distintos, hijos. Cumpliré los encargos de todos.

VIEJO

Muy distintos.

ENRIQUE

¿Qué dices?

VIEJO

¿Te puedo llevar las maletas?

ENRIQUE

No.

[Se oyen risas de niños.]

VIEJO

¿Son hijos tuyos?

ENRIQUE

Los seis.

VIEJO

Yo conozco hace mucho tiempo a la madre de ellos, a tu mujer. Estuve de cochero en su casa; pero si te confieso la verdad, ahora estoy mejor de mendigo. Los caballos, ¡¡jajajá! Nadie sabe el miedo que a mí me dan los caballos. Caiga un rayo sobre todos sus ojos. Guiar un coche es muy difícil. ¡Oh! Es dificilísimo. Si no tienes miedo, no te enteras, y si te enteras, tienes miedo.[2] ¡Malditos sean los caballos!

ENRIQUE

[Cogiendo las maletas.] Déjame.

VIEJO

No, no. Yo, por unas monedillas, las más pequeñas que tengas, te las llevo. Tu mujer te lo agradecerá. Ella no tenía miedo a los caballos. Ella es feliz.

ENRIQUE

You're so different, my children. I'll take care of all your requests.

OLD MAN

So different.

ENRIQUE

What was that?

OLD MAN

Can I carry your bags?

ENRIQUE

No.

[Children's laughter is heard.]

OLD MAN

Are they your children?

ENRIQUE

All six.

OLD MAN

I've known their mother, your wife, for a long time. I was the coachman in her house; but to tell you the truth, I'm better off now as a beggar. Horses, ha ha ha! No one knows how afraid I am of horses. May lightning strike all of them in the eyes. It's hard to drive a coach. Oh! It's so hard. If you're not afraid, you don't realize it, and if you do realize it, you're afraid. Damn all horses!

ENRIQUE

[Taking his bags.] Let me alone.

OLD MAN

No, no. For just a couple coins, the littlest ones you have, I'll carry them for you. Your wife will thank you. She isn't afraid of horses. She is happy.

ENRIQUE

Vamos pronto. A las seis he de tomar el tren.

VIEJO

¡Ah, el tren! Eso es otra cosa. El tren es una tontería. Aunque viviera cien años, yo no tendría miedo al tren. El tren no está vivo. Pasa y ha pasado... Pero los caballos... Mira.

MUJER

[En la ventana.] Enrique mío. Enrique. No dejes de escribirme. No me olvides.

VIEJO

¡Ah, la muchacha! *[Ríe.]* ¿Te acuerdas cómo saltaba la tapia, cómo se subía a los árboles solo por verte?

MUJER

Lo recordaré hasta que muera.

ENRIQUE

Yo también.

MUJER

Te espero. Adiós.

ENRIQUE

Adiós.

VIEJO

No te aflijas. Es tu mujer y te ama. Tú la amas a ella. No te aflijas.

ENRIQUE

Es verdad, pero me pesa esta ausencia...

VIEJO

Peor es otra cosa. Peor es que todo ande y que el río suene. Peor es que haya un ciclón.

ENRIQUE

Let's go quick. I have a six o'clock train to catch.

OLD MAN

Oh, the train! That's another matter. The train is nothing. Even if I lived a hundred years, I'd not be afraid of the train. The train is not alive. It passes and that's the end of it . . . . But horses . . . . Look.

WIFE

[In the window.] Enrique, my Enrique. Make sure you write to me. Don't forget me.

OLD MAN

Ah, the girl! *[Laughs.]* Do you remember how she used to jump the wall, how she climbed into the trees just to see you?

WIFE

I'll remember it until the day I die.

ENRIQUE

So will I.

WIFE

I'll wait for you. Goodbye.

ENRIQUE

Goodbye.

OLD MAN

Don't be sad. She's your wife and she loves you. You love her. Don't be sad.

ENRIQUE

It's true, but this parting weighs on me . . . .

OLD MAN

Worse things could happen. Worse is that everything just happens and the river rolls on. Worse is if there were a hurricane.

ENRIQUE
No tengo ganas de bromas. Siempre estás así.

VIEJO
¡Jajajá! Todo el mundo, y tú el primero, cree que lo importante de un ciclón son los destrozos que produce, y yo creo todo lo contrario. Lo importante de un ciclón...

ENRIQUE
[Irritándose.] Vamos. Van a dar las seis de un momento a otro.

VIEJO
Pues ¿y el mar?... En el mar...

ENRIQUE
[Furioso.] Vamos, he dicho.

VIEJO
¿No se olvida nada?

ENRIQUE
Todo lo dejo perfectamente organizado. Y, además, ¿a tí qué te importa? Lo peor del mundo es un criado viejo, un mendigo.

VOZ 1
Papá.

VOZ 2
Papá.

VOZ 3
Papá.

VOZ 4
Papá.

VOZ 5
Papá.

ENRIQUE

I'm not in the mood for jokes. You're always like this.

OLD MAN

Hahaha! The whole world, and you above all, thinks the important thing about a hurricane is the destruction it causes, and I believe exactly the opposite. The important thing about a hurricane is . . . .

ENRIQUE

[Getting irritated] Get going. It's almost six o'clock already.

OLD MAN

Take the sea . . . . In the sea . . . .

ENRIQUE

[Angry] Get going, I said.

OLD MAN

Have you forgotten anything?

ENRIQUE

I've left everything in perfect order. And anyway, what's it to you? The worst thing in the world is an old servant, a beggar.

1ST VOICE

Papa.

2ND VOICE

Papa.

3RD VOICE

Papa.

4TH VOICE

Papa.

5TH VOICE

Papa.

VOZ 6

Papá.

VIEJO

Tus hijos.

ENRIQUE

Mis hijos.

NIÑA

[En la puerta.] Yo no quiero la ardilla. Si me traes la ardilla, no te querré. No me traigas la ardilla. No la quiero.

VOZ

Ni yo el lagarto.

VOZ

Ni yo el topo.

NIÑA

Queremos que nos traigas una colección de minerales.

VOZ

No, no; yo quiero mi topo.

VOZ

No; el topo es para mí. . .

[Riñen.]

NIÑA

[Entrando.] Pues ahora el topo va a ser para mí.

ENRIQUE

¡Basta! ¡Quedaréis contentos!

6TH VOICE

Papa.

OLD MAN

Your children.

ENRIQUE

My children.

GIRL

[At the door.] I don't want the squirrel. If you bring me the squirrel, I won't love you anymore. Don't bring me the squirrel. I don't want it.

VOICE

Nor I the lizard.

VOICE

Nor I the mole.

GIRL

We want you to bring us a rock collection.

VOICE

No, no; I want my mole.

VOICE

No; the mole is for me . . . .

[They quarrel.]

GIRL

[Entering.] Well now the mole will be for me.

ENRIQUE

Enough! You'll all be happy!

VIEJO
Dijiste que eran muy distintos.

ENRIQUE
Sí. Muy distintos. Afortunadamente.

VIEJO
¿Cómo?

ENRIQUE
[Fuerte.] Afortunadamente.

VIEJO
[Triste.] Afortunadamente.

[Salen.]

MUJER
[En la ventana.] Adiós.

VOZ
Adiós.

MUJER
Vuelve pronto.

VOZ
[Lejana.] Pronto.

MUJER
Se abrigará bien por la noche. Lleva cuatro mantas. Yo, en cambio, estaré sola en la cama. Tendré frío. El tiene ojos maravillosos; pero lo que yo amo es su fuerza. *[Se desnuda.]* Me duele un poco la espalda. ¡Ah! ¡Si me pudiera despreciar! Yo quiero que él me desprecie... y me ame. Yo quiero huir y que me alcance. Yo quiero que me queme..., que me queme. *[Alto.]* Adiós, adiós... Enrique. Enrique... Te amo. Te veo pequeño. Saltas por las piedras. Pequeño. Ahora te podría tragar como si fueras un botón. Te podría tragar, Enrique...

OLD MAN

You were the one who said they were all so different.

ENRIQUE

Yes. So different. Fortunately.

OLD MAN

What?

ENRIQUE

[Forceful] Fortunately.

OLD MAN

[Sad] Fortunately.

  [They exit.]

WIFE

[At the window] Goodbye.

VOICE

Goodbye.

WIFE

See you soon.

VOICE

[Distant] Soon.

WIFE

He'll be cozy at night. He's got four blankets. I, on the other hand, will be alone in bed. I'll be cold. He has marvelous eyes; but what I love is his strength. *[Undresses]* My back hurts a little. Ah! If he would just despise me! I wish he would despise me ... and love me. I want to run and have him catch me. I want him to burn me ..., to burn me. *[Out loud]* Goodbye, good-bye ... Enrique, Enrique ... I love you. I see you getting smaller. You jump from rock to rock. Little. Now I could swallow you like a button. I could swallow you, Enrique ....

NIÑA

Mamá.

MUJER

No salgas. Se ha levantado un viento frio. ¡He dicho que no!
[Entra.]

> *[La luz huye de la escena.]*

NIÑA

[Rápida.] ¡Papáaa! ¡Papáaa! Que me traigas la ardilla. Que yo
no quiero los minerales. Los minerales me romperán las uñas.
Papáaa.

NIÑO

[En la puerta.] No-te-oye. No-te-oye. No-te-oye.

NIÑA

Papá, que yo quiero la ardilla. *[Rompiendo a llorar.]* ¡Dios mío!
¡Yo quiero la ardilla!

Fin

GIRL

Momma.

WIFE

Don't go out. There's a cold wind coming up. I said don't! *[Enters]*

[The light runs from the stage.]

GIRL

[Quickly] Papaaa! Papaaa! Bring me the squirrel! I don't want the rocks. The rocks would break my fingernails. Papaaa!

BOY

[At the door] He-can't-hear-you. He-can't-hear-you. He-can't-hear-you.

GIRL

Papa, I want the squirrel. *[Starting to cry]* My God! I want the squirrel!

End

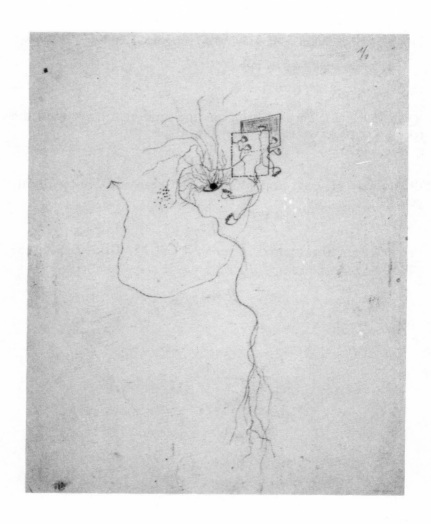

La vista y el tacto [h. 1929-1930]

Sight and Touch

Viaje a la Luna
Trip to the Moon

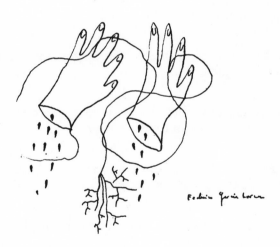

Viaje a la Luna

Guión cinematográfico

1

Cama blanca sobre una pared gris. Sobre los paños surge un baile de números 13 y 22. Desde dos empiezan a surgir hasta que cubren la cama como hormigas diminutas.

2

Una mano invisible arranca los paños.

3

Pies grandes corren rápidamente con exagerados calcetines de rombos blancos y negros.

4

Cabeza asustada que mira fija un punto y se disuelve sobre una cabeza de alambre con un fondo de agua.

5

Letras que digan *"Socorro Socorro Socorro"* con doble exposición sobre un sexo de mujer con movimiento de arriba abajo.

6

Pasillo largo recorrido por la cámara con ventana de final.

7

Vista de Broadway de noche.

8

Se disuelve el todo en la escena anterior.

9

Dos piernas oscilan con gran rapidez.

Trip to the Moon

Screenplay

1

White bed against a gray wall. The numbers 13 and 22 start to dance on top of the blankets. From two, they increase in number until they cover the bed like tiny ants.

2

An invisible hand snatches the blankets off.

3

Huge feet run quickly in exaggerated stockings covered with black and white diamonds.

4

Frightened head staring fixedly at a point and dissolving into a head of wires with water in the background.

5

Letters that read *Help Help Help*, moving up and down, double-exposed over a woman's sex.

6

The camera dollies down a long hall with a window at the end.

7

View of Broadway at night.

8

Dissolve all back to preceding scene.

9

Two legs flash back and forth very quickly.

10

Las piernas se disuelven sobre un grupo de manos que tiemblan.

11

Las manos que tiemblan, sobre una doble exposición de un niño que llora.

12

Y el niño que llora, sobre una doble exposición de una mujer que le da una paliza.

13

Esta escena se disuelve sobre el pasillo largo, que otra vez la cámara recorre hacia atrás con gran rapidez.

14

Al final, un gran plano de un ojo sobre una doble exposición de peces, que se disuelve sobre lo siguiente.

15

Caída rápida. Por una ventana pasa en color azul una doble exposición de letras: "*¡Socorro! ¡Socorro!*..."

16

Cada letrero de "*¡Socorro! ¡Socorro!*" se disuelve en la huella de un pie.

17

Y cada huella de pie, en un gusano de seda sobre una hoja en fondo blanco.

18

De los gusanos de seda sale una gran cabeza muerta, y de la cabeza un cielo con luna.

19

La luna se corta y aparece un dibujo de una cabeza que vomita y abre y cierra los ojos y que se disuelve sobre

20

dos niños que caminan cantando con los ojos cerrados.

21

Cabezas de los niños que cantan llenas de manchas de tinta.

TRIP TO THE MOON o 243

10
Legs dissolve into a group of trembling hands.

11
The trembling hands, double-exposed over a crying child.

12
And the crying child, double-exposed over a woman who is beating him.

13
The scene dissolves into the long hallway, and the camera once more dollies, backwards and very quickly.

14
At the end, a close-up of an eye, double exposed over some fish, that dissolves into the following.

15
Rapid fall. Through a window in double exposure pass the words "*Help! Help!*" ... colored blue.

16
Each of the signs reading "*Help! Help!*" dissolves into a footprint.

17
And each footprint, into a silkworm on a leaf, against a white background.

18
From the silkworms comes a large dead head, and the from head comes a sky with the moon in it.

19
The moon is cut in half and there appears the drawing of a vomiting head that opens and closes its eyes, and that dissolves into

20
Two children who walk along singing, with their eyes closed.

21
Heads full of ink spots of the children singing.

22

Un plano blanco sobre el cual se arrojan gotas de tinta.

23

Puerta.

24

Sale un hombre con una bata blanca. Por el lado opuesto viene un muchacho en traje de baño de grandes manchas blancas y negras.

25

Gran plano del traje sobre una doble exposición de un pez.

26

El hombre de la bata le ofrece un traje de arlequín pero el muchacho rehúsa. Entonces el hombre de la bata lo coge por el cuello, el otro grita, pero el hombre de la bata le tapa la boca con el traje de arlequín.

27

Se disuelve el todo sobre una doble exposición de serpientes, ésto sobre cangrejos y éstos en otros peces, todo con ritmo.
Un pez vivo sostenido por la mano de una persona, en un gran plano, que le aprieta hasta que muere y avanza con la boquita abierta hasta cubrir el objetivo.
Dentro de la boquita del pez aparece un gran plano en el cual saltan, en agonía, dos peces.
Estos se convierten en caleidoscopio en el que cien peces saltan o laten en agonía.[1]

28

Letrero: *Viaje a la Luna*

Habitación. Dos mujeres vestidas de negro lloran sentadas con las cabezas echadas en una mesa donde hay una lámpara. Dirigen las manos al cielo.

29

Planos de los bustos y las manos. Tienen las cabelleras echadas sobre las caras y las manos contrahechas con espirales de alambre.

30

Siguen las mujeres bajando los brazos y subiéndolos al cielo.

22

A white plane on which are thrown drops of ink.

23

Door.

24

Enter a man in a white gown. From the opposite side comes a boy in a bathing suit with big black and white spots.

25

Shot of the bathing suit with double-exposure of a fish.

26

The man in the gown offers him a harlequin's costume, but the boy refuses it. Then the man in the white gown grabs him by the neck, the other cries out, but the man in the gown covers his mouth with the harlequin's costume.

27

Dissolve all into a double exposure of snakes, this into crabs and these into fish, all in rhythm.

Close-up of a live fish held in someone's hand, who squeezes it until it dies and advances with the little open mouth until it covers the lens.

Inside the fish's mouth, a shot in which two fish jump in agony. These change into a kaleidoscope where a hundred fish jump or undulate in agony.

28

Title: *Trip to the Moon*

Room. Two women dressed in black sit and cry with their heads on a table where there is a lamp. They raise their hands to the sky.

29

Shots of their busts and their hands. Their hair is fallen over their faces and their fake hands are made with spirals of wire.

30

The women go on lowering their hands and lifting them to the sky.

31

Una rana cae sobre la mesa.

32

Doble exposición de la rana vista enorme sobre un fondo de orquídeas agitadas con furia.

Se van las orquídeas y aparece una cabeza enorme dibujada de mujer que vomita que cambia de negativo a positivo y de positivo a negativo rápidamente.

Una puerta se cierra violentamente y otra puerta y otra y otra sobre una doble exposición de las mujeres que suben y bajan los brazos. Al cerrarse cada puerta saldrá un letrero que diga . . . *"Elena Helena, elhena elHeNa."*

33

Las mujeres se dirigen rápidamente a la puerta.

34

La cámara baja con gran ritmo acelerado las escaleras y con doble exposición las sube.

35

Triple exposición de subir y bajar escaleras.

36

Doble exposición de barrotes que pasan sobre un dibujo: "Muerte de Santa Radegunda."

37

Una mujer enlutada se cae por la escalera.

38

Gran plano de ella.

39

Otra vista de ella muy realista. Lleva pañuelo en la cabeza a la manera española. Exposición de las narices echando sangre.

40

Cabeza boca abajo de ella con doble exposición sobre un dibujo de venas y granos gordos de sal para el relieve.

31

A frog falls on the table.

32

Double exposure of the frog, made huge, on a background of furiously waving orchids.

The orchids go away and there appears a huge outline of a woman vomiting, which quickly changes from negative to positive and from positive to negative.

A door is slammed shut, and another door and another and another against a double exposure of the women who lift and lower their arms. As each door closes there will emerge a title that reads . . . *"Elena Helena, elhena elHeNa."*

33

The women go quickly to the door.

34

The camera descends the stairs in greatly accelerated rhythm, and in double exposure climbs them.

35

Triple exposure of ascending and descending the stairs.

36

Double exposure of window bars passing over a drawing of "The Death of Santa Radegunda".

37

A woman in mourning falls down the stairs.

38

Close-up of her.

39

Another view of her, very realistic. She wears a scarf in her hair, after the Spanish manner. View of her nostrils bleeding.

40

Her face-down head in double exposure over a drawing of veins and big grains of salt, in relief.

41

La cámara desde abajo enfoca y sube la escalera. En lo alto aparece un desnudo de muchacho. Tiene la cabeza como los muñecos anatómicos con los músculos y las venas y los tendones. Luego sobre el desnudo lleva dibujado el sistema de la circulación de la sangre y arrastra un traje de arlequín.

42

Aparece de medio cuerpo.

43

Y mira de un lado a otro. Se disuelve en una calle nocturna.

44

Ya en la calle nocturna hay tres tipos con gabanes que dan muestras de frío . . . Llevan los cuellos subidos. Uno mira la luna hacia arriba levantando la cabeza y aparece la luna en la pantalla, otro mira la luna y aparece una cabeza de pájaro en gran plano a la cual se estruja el cuello hasta que muera ante el objetivo, el tercero mira la luna y aparece en la pantalla una luna dibujada sobre fondo blanco que se disuelve sobre un sexo y el sexo en la boca que grita.

45

Huyen los tres por la calle.

46

Aparece en la calle el hombre de las venas y queda en cruz.
Avanza en saltos de pantalla.

47

Se disuelve sobre un cruce en triple exposición de trenes rápidos.

48

Los trenes se disuelven sobre una doble exposición de teclados de piano y manos tocando.

49

Se disuelve sobre un bar donde hay varios muchachos vestidos de smoking. El camarero les echa vino pero no pueden llevarlo a su boca. Los vasos se hacen pesadísimos y luchan en una angustia de sueño. Entra una muchacha casi desnuda y un arlequín y bailan en ralenti. Todos prueban a beber pero no pueden. El camarero llena sin cesar los vasos que ya están llenos.

41

The camera, from below, focuses on the stairs and climbs them. Above, there appears the nude of a boy. He has the head of an anatomist's model, with the muscles and the veins and the tendons showing. And on the nude is drawn the vascular system, and it drags a harlequin's costume.

42

Appears from the waist up.

43

And looks from one side to the other. Dissolve into a street at night.

44

On the street at night there are three fellows with overcoats who show signs of being cold . . . . Their collars are turned up. One looks up at the moon, lifting his head, and the moon appears on the screen; another looks at the moon, and there appears the head of bird, in close-up, whose neck is wrung until it dies before the lens; the third looks at the moon, and there appears on the screen a drawing of a moon against a white background, that dissolves into a man's sex, and the sex into a screaming mouth.

45

The three flee down the street.

46

The man with the veins appears in the street and stops with arms extended.
He comes forward in fast motion.

47

Dissolve into a railroad crossing with a triple exposure of speeding trains.

48

The trains dissolve into a double exposure of piano keys and hands playing.

49

Dissolve to a bar where there are several boys dressed in smoking jackets. The waiter pours them wine, but they can't bring it to their mouths. The glasses become very heavy and they struggle in the anguish of dream. Enter an almost naked girl and a harlequin and they dance in slow motion. All of them try to drink but they can't. The waiter keeps filling the glasses that are already full.

50

Aparece el hombre de las venas gesticulante y haciendo señas desesperadas y movimientos que expresan vida y ritmo acelerado. Todos los hombres se quedan adormilados.

51

Una cabeza mira estúpidamente. Se acerca a la pantalla. Y se disuelve en una rana. El hombre de las venas estruja la rana con los dedos.

52

Sale una esponja y una cabeza vendada.

53

Se disuelve sobre una calle donde una muchacha vestida de blanco huye con un arlequín.

54

Una cabeza que vomita.
Y en seguida toda la gente del bar vomita.

55

Se disuelve lo anterior sobre un ascensor donde un negrito también vomita.

56

El muchacho arlequín y la mujer desnuda suben en el ascensor.

57

Se abrazan.
Plano de un beso sensual.

58

El muchacho muerde a la muchacha en el cuello y tira violentamente de sus cabellos.

59

Aparece una guitarra y una mano rápidamente corta las cuerdas con unas tijeras.

60

La muchacha se defiende del muchacho y éste, con gran furia, le da otro beso profundo y pone los dedos pulgares sobre los ojos, como para hundirlos en ellos.

50

The man with the veins appears gesturing and making desperate signs and movements that express life and accelerated rhythm. All the men have fallen asleep.

51

A head looks on stupidly. It approaches the screen. And dissolves to a frog. The man with the veins squeezes the frog between his fingers.

52

Enter a sponge and a bandaged head.

53

Dissolve into a street where a girl dressed in white runs off with a harlequin.

54

A vomiting head.
And immediately everyone in the bar vomits.

55

The preceeding dissolves to an elevator where a little black boy also vomits.

56

The boy harlequin and the naked woman ride up in the elevator.

57

They embrace.
Shot of a sensual kiss.

58

The boy bites the girl on her neck and violently pulls her hair.

59

A guitar appears, and a hand quickly cuts the strings with a pair of scissors.

60

The girl defends herself from the boy and he, with great fury, gives her another deep kiss and puts his index fingers over her eyes, as though to sink them into their sockets.

61

Grita la muchacha y el muchacho, de espaldas, se quita la americana y una peluca y aparece el hombre de las venas.

62

Entonces ella se disuelve en un busto de yeso blanco y el hombre de las venas la besa apasionadamente.

63

Se ve el busto de yeso con huellas de labios y huellas de manos.

64

Vuelven a salir las palabras *"Elena elena elena elena."*

65

Estas palabras se disuelven sobre grifos que echan agua de manera violenta.

66

Y estos grifos sobre el hombre de las venas muerto sobre periódicos abandonados y arenques.

67

Aparece una cama y unas manos que cubren un muerto.

68

Viene un muchacho con una bata blanca y guantes de goma y una muchacha vestida de negro. Pintan un bigote con tinta a una cabeza terrible de muerto. Y se besan con grandes risas.

69

De ellos surge un cementerio y se les ve besarse sobre una tumba.

70

Plano de un beso cursi de cine con otros personajes.

71

Y al final con prisa la luna y árboles con viento.

Fin

61

The girl screams and the boy, his back to us, removes his jacket and a wig, and appears as the man with the veins.

62

Then she dissolves to a white plaster bust and the man with the veins kisses her passionately.

63

The plaster bust is seen with tracks of kisses and hand prints.

64

Again appear the words, *"Elena elena elena elena."*

65

These words dissolve to faucets that spout water violently.

66

And these faucets, to the man with the veins dead on top of old newspapers and sardines.

67

A bed appears, and hands that cover a corpse.

68

Along comes a boy in a white coat and rubber gloves and a girl dressed in black. With ink, they draw a mustache on a terrible death's-head. And they kiss with great laughter.

69

A cemetery rises around them and they are seen kissing on top of a tomb.

70

Shot of a fake-elegant screen kiss with other characters in the background.

71

And at the end hurriedly the moon and trees in wind.

End

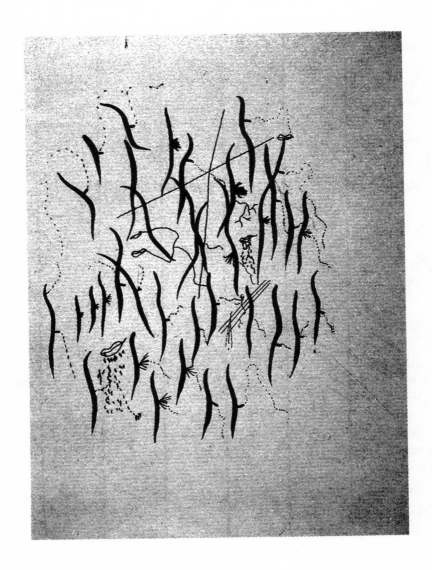

Bosque sexual [h. 1933]

Sexual Forest

Textual Sources

We consulted the following editions and manuscripts of *Así que pasen cinco años* in our preparation of the edition and translation. Each is listed with the abbreviation used to identify it in the Notes.

OC: Obras Completas, volume II, 18th edition. Madrid: Aguilar, 1974.

LO: Así que pasen cinco años, 3rd edition. Buenos Aires: Losada, 1968.

AU: "Así que pasen cinco años," *Autógrafos*, volume III, edited by Rafael Martínez Nadal. Oxford, England: The Dolphin Book Co., 1979. A facsimile of the manuscript in possession of Rafael Martinez Nadal.

CA: Club Anfistora typewritten manuscript, in possession of Margarita Ucelay, with handwritten corrections in Lorca's hand.

Muerte de Santa Rodegunda [1929]

Death of Santa Rodegunda

Notes

Introduction

1. Marcelle Auclair, *Enfance et Mort de García Lorca*. (Paris: Editions du Seuil, 1968), p. 236–237.
2. Eutimio Martín, *Federico García Lorca, Heterodoxo y Mártir*. (Madrid: Siglo XXI Editores, 1986).
3. Francisco García Lorca, *In the Green Morning, Memories of Federico* (translated by Christopher Maurer). (New York: New Directions, 1986), p. 35.
4. Andre Belamich (ed), *Suites*. (Barcelona: Editorial Ariel, 1983).
5. Christopher Maurer (ed), "Federico García Lorca escribe a su familia desde New York y la Habana," *Poesia: Revista ilustrada de informacion poetica*, no. 23–24. no date, p. 133–141.
6. First published by Christopher Maurer in "Sobre la prosa temprana de Federico García Lorca," *Cuadernos Hispanoamericanos*, 433–436 (Julio-octubre 1986), p. 16.

Once Five Years Pass (Legend of Time)
Act One

1. *OC* and *LO* add "en tres actos y cinco cuadros."
2. *OC* and *LO*. "Characters" is followed by a list, in order of appearance: "EL JOVEN, EL VIEJO, LA MECANOGRAFA, EL AMIGO, EL NIÑO, EL GATO, EL CRIADO, AMIGO 2, LA NOVIA, EL JUGADOR DE RUGBY, LA CRIADA, EL PADRE, EL MANIQUI, ARLEQUIN, LA MUCHACHA, EL PAYASO, LA MASCARA, LA CRIADA, JUGADOR 1, JUGADOR 2, JUGADOR 3, EL ECO."
3. Though the original manuscript has "EL JUGADOR DE RUGBY," we have translated it as "THE FOOTBALL PLAYER." Lorca clearly meant to define the character as a player of American football, a game that resembles European rugby, and to avoid the confusion of using the simple word "futbol," which in Spanish refers to soccer. Lorca himself used the term "rugby" for American foot-

ball in a letter written to his family from New York: "Ahora mismo sale al campo el equipo de rugby de Columbia, vestido de negro y tabaco. Los jugadores tienen cualidades de papel de lija y tronco de árbol; algo de una fortaleza y una sordidez que asusta." A little later in the same letter, he adds, "Es un juego que me gusta mucho, el rugby, y que además de ser típicamente americano, tiene una emoción y una belleza *natural* increíble, hasta que no se paladea bien. Claro que yo no hubiera sido jamás jugador." And in a later letter, he writes, "También voy a los partidos de rugby que se celebran en el Stadium de la Universidad. Anteayer hubo cuatro jugadores que perdieron el conocimiento. Pero yo me explico el apasionamiento de la gente porque el juego es hermosísimo, de una virilidad y una agilidad al mismo tiempo que cautiva al débil que no lo puede hacer." [*F.G.L. escribe a su familia desde Nueva York y La Habana 1929–1930*, edited by Christopher Maurer. Revista Poesía, no. 23–24. (Madrid: Ministerio de Cultura, 1985).]

4. *OC* and *LO*. "No se sorprende."

5. *LO* adds "Y es curioso: ¿no la ve usted destacarse sobre un cielo claro de alba?" In the manuscript, the brief section beginning "Es una palabra verde" and ending with the above-cited is underlined and enclosed within a sort of brackets, as though for a possible cut. During the rehearsals for the premiere, Lorca did cut only the latter part, as can be seen in *CA*.

6. Two variants of the same sentence are crossed-out in the manuscript: "Todo permanece intacto." and "Las cosas permanecen intactas."

7. What follows in the text, up to Note 13, constitutes our edition of three pages of manuscript that have been wrongly placed since the first typewritten copy of the play. As a result of the wrong placement, it has been difficult to understand the unfolding of the most important moment in the first scene, where the title of the work appears in dialogue for the first time. This wrong placement has been perpetuated in all published editions of the work up to now. The error, which we rectify in this edition, occurred because there is a page in the manuscript that is missing its upper righthand corner, where the page number would have been written. Since it was collated directly after the page numbered 3, the typist continued entering text as though this were the proper page to follow page 3. This is not possible, however, because there also exists in the manuscript a page numbered 4, whose dialogue fits perfectly with the dialogue that concludes page 3. Furthermore, page 3 ends with a question of the VIEJO and the unnumbered page begins with an answer from the VIEJO, while at the same time, the unnumbered page ends with a speech of the JOVEN and page 4 begins with another speech of the JOVEN; as a result, the dialogue that occurs

in these pages seems garbled and illogical. We deduced, therefore, that the numberless page must have been an insert that Lorca made for inclusion on one of the correctly numbered pages, and we discovered that, indeed, on page 4, there is a line extending toward the righthand margin that seems to cross out, but in fact, we believe, is meant to underline the phrase "aquí alusiones al argumento." Furthermore, this line and phrase are written in ink, while the rest of the manuscript is written in pencil. We inserted the numberless page at this position in page 4, and we discovered that the dialogue then flowed with perfect logic.

As a final argument in favor of our decision, we point out that at no other point in the manuscript does Lorca end one page with the name of a character and begin the following page with the name of the same character, when this character is simply continuing a single speech. In such cases, the speech always continues without mention of the name of the character, which had already appeared in its proper place on the preceding page. For this reason, we think it highly unlikely that in this single case, as we mentioned above, two supposedly consecutive pages should end and begin with speeches headed the VIEJO and two more with speeches headed the JOVEN.

8. This response of the JOVEN, "Yo espero," with which page 4 of the manuscript begins, fits perfectly with the question that the VIEJO asks at the end of page 3, "¿De manera que usted? . . . "

9. In the manuscript, the beginning of this speech is crossed out: "Cuando se quiere de verdad, cuando el amor llega hasta la planta de los pies, se espera siempre."

10. Beneath the word "Nunca" in the manuscript, the word "Ayer" is crossed out. Here is where the penned line we referred to in note 7 occurs, making it difficult to read easily the marginal notation "aquí alusiones al argumento," which undoubtedly refers to the insertion of the unnumbered manuscript pages. See note 7.

11. *OC* and *LO* omit the stage direction "*[irónico]*." *OC* and *CA* add, for a second time, "De astronomía."

12. *OC* omits "Las cosas requieren tiempo." and the three speeches that follow it. And here, it adds "VIEJO: ¿Vino el padre de ella?"

13. *OC* has "¡Nunca!"
Crossed out here in the manuscript, the speech of the "VIEJO. —¿Y qué?" This is followed by the speech of the "JOVEN. —Nada . . . ," which, as can be seen, are the two last speeches of the unnumbered pages: "VIEJO.—¿Pero que . . ., JOVEN.—Nada . . ." so that the dialogue of page 4 of the manuscript fits perfectly with the insertion of the unnumbered page. See note 7.

14. Phrase added in *CA*.

15. *AU* and *LO* add "VIEJO. – ¡Es tan hermoso esperar!" and "JOVEN. – Sí, esperar, pero ¡tener! *[Con apasionamiento].*" These are absent in *CA* and *OC*.
    The following is crossed out in the manuscript:
    "VIEJO. – Y hay que vivir apartando los juncos de esta hora que nos rodea en espera del agua que está detrás pero que nos llama y es nuestra.
    JOVEN. – ¡Y no importa la sed!
    VIEJO. – *[Con sorna]* ¡Pero va usted a hablarme a mí de la sed! No hay nada más fácil que jugar con ella o sustituirla. –Deme un cocktail–.
    JOVEN. – Sí. *[Agarra una cocktelera y empieza a hacerlo.]*"

16. *LO*. "Los aires."

17. *OC* and *LO* use a question mark.

18. In the manuscript this speech begins, "No me gusta esa manera de expresar." *OC*, *LO* and *CA* omit it.

19. In *AU*, *OC* and *LO* these phrases end with question marks.

20. *OC* and *LO* omit from the stage directions "Se sienta y."

21. In *AU*, *OC*, and *LO* this phrase ends with a question mark.

22. In the manuscript, the following is crossed out: " ¡Ya lo sé!" From "Pero ya . . ." until "en burbujas," is enclosed in a sort of brackets in the manuscript, as an indication of a possible cut.

23. *OC* and *LO* have "esperar." In the manuscript, "esperar" is crossed out and "aguardar" is written above it, to avoid the inelegance of "esperar . . . en espera."

24. *OC*, *LO* and *AU* have "apagado."

25. *OC* omits "mi."

26. "Perdóname" is crossed out in the manuscript.

27. *CA* adds the stage direction "*[Condescendiente].*"

28. *OC* and *LO* omit the stage direction "*[Se levanta].*" *LO* has "¡Piensa tanto!"

29. *OC*, *LO* and *AU* have "Todo hacia dentro. Una quemadura." *LO* has "adentro."

30. This stage direction is not in the manuscript. It appears in *OC*, *LO* and *CA*.

31. In the manuscript, between a sort of brackets to indicate a possible cut, is the following: "en un cielo sujeto por enormes trenzas de nieve que de pronto se convierten en siemprevivas o en unas cadenas largas amarradas sobre el agua del mar. Es muy fácil que se le afile la nariz y que la mano que lleva sobre el pecho se le ponga como

cinco tallos verdes de sauco por donde van los caracoles." In *CA*, Lorca cut from "que de pronto" until "caracoles.," which is the way that the speech appears in *OC*. *LO* includes the cut material, but omits from "que de pronto" until "mar." and also omits "de sauco."

32. *OC*, *LO* and *AU* have "apartara."

33. In the manuscript, "¿ha visto usted?" is crossed out.

34. *OC* and *LO* omit "Pues si me pongo a pensar en ella . . . "

35. *OC* and *LO* omit "monstruosa."

36. "¡quién!" is underlined in the manuscript.

37. *LO* has "sin resistencia bajo."

38. In the manuscript, the following is crossed out: "Una hoja amarilla, una sección de peces, una rama que alarga el cuello para beber . . . ," and in the following speech of the JOVEN, the words "Exactamente." and "Verdaderamente." are also crossed out.

39. *OC* and *LO* omit "Mire usted."

40. *OC* and *LO* omit this speech and the one following it.

41. *OC* and *LO* have "cambiado."

42. In the manuscript, the following is crossed out: "con toda la cara llena de florecitas!"

43. *OC* and *LO* omit "¡y vamos arriba!, ¡a volar!"

44. "Ahora mismo" is underlined in the manuscript.

45. *OC* and *LO* have "La de siempre." *LO* omits "No se asombre usted." *OC* has "No se asuste usted, ¡señor!" *OC* and *LO* put the stage direction "*[Al VIEJO]*" after the phrase "Cuando pequeñito."

46. In the manuscript, the word "latiendo" is crossed out.

47. "Un cock-tail." is underlined in the manuscript. *OC* and *LO* have "O un cocktail."

48. In the manuscript, the following is crossed out:
"AMIGO. – *[Lo suelta y recita dándole golpecitos en el hombro]*
La llamita de San Juan
por las hojas, por las ramas
corriendo volando va.
¿Te disgustas?
JOVEN. –"

49. In the manuscript, the beginning of this speech is crossed out: "Pobre . . . ¿te hice daño? . . . ¡pero no! ¡no señor!"

50. "Zás" is added in *CA*.

51. In the manuscript, the following is crossed out: "AMIGO.- ¿Qué decías? JOVEN. – Nada."

52. *OC* and *LO* omit "los labios vueltos, *[se levanta]*" In the manuscript, Lorca placed between a sort of brackets, to indicate a possible cut, from "Ernesti-ti-ti-ti-ti-ti-tina" until "con los ojos . . . " *OC* omits it. We have restored it, because we feel it is both very theatrical and crucial to the erotic definition of the AMIGO's personality, which will later be projected onto the JUGADOR DE RUGBY, in contrast to the JOVEN's.

53. In the manuscript, the following is crossed out: "Por estar con Ernestina dejo a otras cuatro. Yo quisiera ser cuatro pero me resigno, . . . o es que tú quizá sabes . . . JOVEN. – Bebe."

54. *OC* and *LO* omit "¿lo oyes?, ja, ja, ja, feísima."
OC and *LO* have "pero admirable."

55. In the manuscript, the following is crossed out: "sabe hacer un refresco de naranja como nadie del mundo."

56. In the manuscript, the two following speeches are crossed out:
"AMIGO. – Los hombros son estupendos; típicos de domador de caballos.
JOVEN. – ¡No te quieres callar! *[Irritado] [con dulzura]*."

57. In the manuscript, "¿qué sabes tú?" is crossed out.

58. In the manuscript, the rest of this speech is crossed out:
"*[Abstraído]* A la derecha de la puerta habrá un mueble alto con libros y luego al fondo el jarrón . . . pero si el tono amarillo de la pared . . . ¡no quiero que sea verde! sino amarillo claro . . . ¡verde no! ¿quién pinta de verde mi casa sin permiso mío? y ella bajará la escalera . . . "
Also, in the succeeding speech of the AMIGO, the following is crossed out:
"*[que ha estado bebiendo – habla al mismo tiempo – y va recordando los componentes del cock-tail chascando la lengua y cantando la escala]* Gin-coñac- cointreau- cherry- sol- la- si- do- jerez. *[Dirigiéndose al JOVEN]*."

59. In the manuscript, "Yo soy feliz." is crossed out.

60. *OC* and *LO* have "¿No conoces mi temperamento?" In the manuscript, the two following speeches are crossed out:
"AMIGO. – ¡Ay pobre! ¿Por qué te alejas tanto de tu niñez? ¿Dónde vas con esa cabeza?
JOVEN. – Hacia adelante. Si las puertas están cerradas yo las golpeo desde aquí, para que cuando llegue ya estén abiertas."

61. *OC* and *LO* have "Yo no lo entiendo." and omit the second "No entiendo."

62. *OC* and *LO* have "le golpea." In the manuscript, the following is crossed out:

"Recotín recotán
La llamita de San Juan
Por las hojas por las ramas
corriendo volando va
Recotín. Recotán."

63. *OC* and *LO* have "Son truenos; tendrás que oirlos."

64. In the manuscript, "irritado" is crossed out in the stage directions.
Before the phrase "debajo de tu cama.," a word beginning "dent"
[*dentro?*] has been crossed out, along with all of the following:
"Una cosa te digo. Hay dos hormigas en tu jardín que serán, las
dueñas de tu lengua no; que son, las dueñas de tu lengua,
JOVEN. – *[Furioso]* Calla
AMIGO. – . . . Que se dormirán sobre las niñas de tus ojos."

65. *OC* adds "Me quieren ustedes decir . . ."

66. In the manuscript, this stage direction, read as follows, before
Lorca's deletions: "Los tres personajes se sitúan a la izquierda y
siguen una discusión apasionada y muda. A veces se sentarán y otras
leerán los tres en un libro o Los tres personajes se ocultarán detrás
de un biombo negro bordado con estrellas. según el ritmo y el juego
de las escenas." Lorca crossed out the first alternative, and also the
phrase that follows "estrellas."

67. *OC* and *LO* add "blanco." In the manuscript, "blanco" is crossed
out.

68. In the manuscript, "en mi alma" is crossed out.

69. In the manuscript, the two following verses are crossed out:
"y la tarde sentada en el tejado
con ramas de coral me iluminaba."

70. *OC* and *LO* have the stage direction "*[Cruzando las manos]*,"
whereas, as can be seen further on, this is the stage direction that
introduces the song "Ay girasol" and that appears further on in the
text. In the manuscript, the following is crossed out:
"No vinieron los an
[cruzando las manos] Ay girasol
Ay girasol de fuego
Ay girasol
GATO. – ¡Ay clavellina del sol!
NIÑO. – Apagado va por el cielo
solo mares y montes y carbón
y una paloma muerta por la arena
con las alas tronchadas y en el pico una flor
[canta] Y en la flor una oliva
y en la oliva un limón
. . . ."

¿cómo sigue . . ? ¡no lo sé! ¿cómo sigue?
GATO. – ¡Ay girasol de la mañanita! ay girasol
No hay luz ¿dónde estás niño?"

71. In the manuscript, the two following verses are crossed out:
"NIÑO. – Perdóname si estuve algo incorrecto.
GATO. – Estuviste muy guapo. niño ¡Gracias!"

72. *OC* adds "te."

73. *OC* has "aprisionaron." *LO* has "hirieron."

74. *OC* adds "los." *LO* omits the "o."

75. *OC* has "recoger."

76. *OC* and *LO* omit the question mark. In the manuscript, the phrase
"¿Sin nadie?" can be read quite clearly beneath "¡Qué miedo!,"
which is crossed out.

77. In the manuscript, the following verses are crossed out:
"Una niña muy grande con zapatos de hebilla
me besaba así, mira, *[besa al gato]*
me estrujaba
cuando todos los niños estaban escondidos
debajo de los juncos por donde llora el agua."

78. *LO* omits from "Y después a la Iglesia" until "chupar monedas."

79. *LO* has "Siempre lirios."

80. *OC* and *LO* have "*[Le toma de la pata]*."

81. In the manuscript, "muy grandes" is crossed out.

82. *OC* and *AU* have "hijitos pequeños."

83. *OC*, *LO* and *AU* have "las patitas."

84. *OC*, *LO* and *AU* have "las nubes."

85. *OC* and *LO* have "ni el viento."

86. *OC* and *LO* have "clavelina." *OC* has "por el cielo."

87. *OC* and *LO* have "*[EL NIÑO y LA GATA, agarrados]*."

88. *OC* and *LO* have "*[Dentro]* ¡Niño!, ¡niño!, ¡niño! *[Con angustia]* ¡Niño!, ¡niño!*"

89. In the manuscript, "NO" is written in capital letters. *OC* has "No,
no.," and adds a speech as follows: "NIÑO. – Siempre dije que no."

90. The word "será" is underlined in the manuscript.

91. In the manuscript, beneath the word "escapar," the word "zafar"
has been crossed out. After "tormenta.," the following is crossed
out: "Me repugna el hombre que echa las monedas de oro en la
alcantarilla.
JOVEN. – Y a mí me repugna el que las tiene."

92. *OC* and *LO* add "y," which is clearly crossed out in the manuscript.

93. In the manuscript, "hijo" is crossed out.

94. In the manuscript, "VIEJO" is underlined.

95. *LO* has "tendrá." *OC* has "las llaves."

96. In the manuscript, "muchachos" is crossed out. Also, after "quitarlo," the phrase "de allí" is crossed out.

97. *OC* and *LO* have "No podía usted con él."

98. In the manuscript, at this point, the following speech is crossed out: "VIEJO. – *[Severamente]* Ya lo oye usted."

99. In the manuscript, the following is crossed out: "¿No es mucho más hermoso que retorcer el cuello a la paloma llenarse de trigo la mano y cogerla cuando ella se acerque a comer?"

100. Lorca put a sort of brackets in the manuscript from "JOVEN. – Esperando . . . " until "AMIGO.- . . . mi solapa.," to indicate a possible cut. Indeed, the section has been lightly crossed out in pencil with a very indistinct line. It might be argued that the speech of the VIEJO, "¡No es verdad!" is most clearly a rejection of the preceding affirmation of the AMIGO, "¡Primero eres tú que los demás!"

101. In the manuscript, "la gente" is crossed out.

102. *OC* and *LO* have "¿Recuerda usted?"

103. In the manuscript, "perfectamente" is crossed out.

104. This is identical to the poem entitled "El regreso," that Lorca had written in 1921 as part of the *Suites*. *OC* and *LO* repeat both times the phrase "dejadme volver" and lump together in one line several that were originally written in two.

105. *OC* and *LO* have "precisamente."

106. *OC* and *LO* have "con." In the manuscript "a" is crossed out. In the following sentence, preceding "robado," the words "aquí" and "cada hora" are crossed out.

107. *OC* and *LO* omit the stage direction "*[Sereno]*."

108. The phrase "ha pasado" is underlined in the manuscript.

109. In the manuscript, the following two sentences, useful for understanding the AMIGO 2's speech, are crossed out: "Ese niño que he visto muerto lo despertaré luego y me despertaré a mí mismo dándome muchos golpes para jugar al caballo caballito."

110. *OC* and *LO* have "*[Serio y con honradez]*."

111. *OC* and *LO* make them affirmatives: "Sí, sí."

112. *OC* and *LO* have "*[bebe rápidamente las copas, apurando hasta lo último.]*"

113. *OC* and *LO* omit "en medio de una alegrísima sonrisa." In the manuscript, beneath "sonrisa," the word "carcajada" is crossed out.

114. We have added "se," because we believe that this is the movement called for by the speech that follows.

115. *OC* adds "No te había llamado."

116. *OC*, *LO* and *AU* have "dejadme tornar." We prefer to leave the phrase the same as it was in its previous occurrence, "¡dejadme retornar!"

Act Two

1. *LO* has "Tiene una larga cola y todo el cabello en bucles." *OC* has "cabello lleno de bucles."

2. See note 3 of Act One. *OC* and *LO* have "Lleva una bolsa llena de cigarros puros."

3. *OC* and *LO* have "aplasta en el piso el cigarro."

4. *OC* and *LO* add "con los cascos."

5. *OC* and *LO* have "*[Le abraza]*."

6. *LO* has "y puedes romperme." In the manuscript, the following is crossed out: "*[EL JUGADOR DE RUGBY la besa en la boca]* Tus besos me caen en la boca como un puñado de oro caliente que sale de pronto de la tierra." There is some doubt as to whether this cut is by Lorca himself, since it is made in pencil, while other cuts in the same scene are made in pen, using the same ink as that in which this part of the text is written. Might this have been an example of censorship, given the erotic character of the image?

7. *OC* has "*[pasandole la mano por el cuello.]*"

8. Added in *OC* and *CA*.

9. In the manuscript, the speech that followed is crossed out: "JUGADOR. – *[Con un gruñido]* Sí."

10. *OC* has "un cigarro puro." *LO* has "otro cigarro."

11. *OC* and *LO* have "Mi novio."

12. *OC* and *LO* have "como labios secos."

13. In the manuscript, the following is crossed out: "Anoche ví un niño muy pequeño sobre el tocador. Tenía rodilleras como tú, y arrugas de cuero por la cabeza, pero no eran de cuero, eran de un tejido rosa y luego lo volví a ver en el espejo de mano." In all of this, the only words not crossed out are "y luego lo."

14. Note the possible double meaning in this whole scene with respect to the verb "irse," which can have a sexual meaning.

15. In the manuscript "¡Hasta mañana!" is crossed out, perhaps so as not to lose the double meaning that we alluded to in the previous note.

16. *OC* and *LO* have "alzándola."

17. *OC* and *LO* have "¡Abre!"

18. *OC* and *LO* have "Discuten mucho."

19. *OC* and *LO* use a question mark.

20. *OC* and *LO* omit the stage direction "*[Irónica]*."

21. *OC* has "Este ramo de flores."

22. *OC* and *LO* have "Tíralas por el balcón."

23. *OC* and *LO* have "*[La CRIADA arroja por el balcón unas flores que estaban sobre un jarro.]*"

24. *OC* and *LO* have "en lo que va a hacer!"

25. *OC*, *LO* and *AU* invert the order, "Tanto tiempo esperándola. Con tanta ilusión." And *OC* adds "Cinco años." only once.

26. *OC* and *LO* omit the stage direction "*[Con sorna]*." In the manuscript, the two following speeches are crossed out in pencil: "CRIADA. – ¡Los señores son más finos! NOVIA. – ¡O más de nieve!"

27. *OC* and *LO* omit the stage direction "*[Irritada]*."

28. *OC* and *LO* have "Con el rojo."

29. *OC* and *LO* omit the stage direction "*[Suave]*" and put a question mark in "¿El naranja?," "¿El de tules?," and "¿El traje de hojas de otoño?" Likewise, they place the stage directions after the negative answers of the NOVIA.

30. *OC* and *CA* have added "para ese hombre."

31. *OC* and *LO* have "buscaba."

32. In the manuscript, there follow these two speeches, which were cut in *CA*: "CRIADA. – *[Sorprendida]* ¡Ay señorita! NOVIA. – Díme."

33. *OC* and *LO* omit these two phrases.

34. In the manuscript, the following two speeches are crossed out: "NOVIA. – ¿No sería que lo regalaría a otra? CRIADA. –¿Cómo iba a hacer eso?"

35. *OC* has "Allí." In the manuscript, "¡Su padre!" has been crossed out, and written above it in pencil is "Ahí llega su padre."

36. Added in *CA*.

37. *OC* and *LO* have "con razón."

38. The word "hermoso" is added in *OC* and *CA*, as is the sentence, "Ahí dentro está, en el maniquí."

39. In the manuscript, "NO" is written in capital letters, as it was at the end of the scene of the Boy and the Cat in Act One.

40. *OC* and *LO* have "Ya han apagado las lámparas. *[Con angustia]* ¡Será hermoso!" In the manuscript, the phrase "¡Será hermoso!" seems to have been placed before "Ya han apagado las lámparas." Furthermore, this seems the more logical order. *OC* has "Y ahora yo no lo veo."

41. *OC* and *LO* have "Ustedes me perdonen."

42. *OC* and *LO* have "¡Le va a oir!"

43. In the manuscript, the following phrase has been crossed out: "Antes siempre estaba quieto."

44. *OC* and *LO* have "No, no."

45. *OC* and *LO* have "garza."

46. *OC* and *LO* have "*[Con energía]*."

47. *OC* has "podría."

48. *LO* has "corriendo."

49. *AU* has "deshaciéndose."

50. In the manuscript follows the sentence, "Yo estoy defendida por el tejado," which has been crossed out in *CA*. *OC*, *LO*, and *AU* have "Aquí no se sueña. Yo no quiero soñar." We have inverted the order of the two preceding phrases so that the dialogue flows more smoothly into the speech that follows.

51. "¡NO!" is written in capital letters in the manuscript.

52. See Note 13 of Act Two.

53. In the manuscript, the following is crossed out: "JOVEN. – La casa está pintada de amarillo para que brillen más tus ojos, para ver tus manos y la sombra de tus manos."

54. In the manuscript, the following is crossed out: "Porque me he roto la frente sobre un muro."

55. *OC* and *LO* have "mala."

56. *OC* and *LO* have "*[Entrando]*."

57. Between these two exclamations, in the manuscript, occurs the following: "NOVIA. – Hay alguien que no debe enterarse de lo que has hecho." It is cut in *CA*.

58. In the manuscript, the following is crossed out: "¡Está empezando el eclipse!" VIEJO. – *[Entrando pálido y vacilante]*."

59. *OC* has "el chico."

60. *OC* has "nuevos."

61. *OC* and *CA* have added "en el maniquí."

62. In the manuscript, the following is crossed out: "*[Con angustia]* ¿Tendré tiempo?"

63. A reference to the eclipse. See note 58, Act Two.

64. *OC* and *LO* have "va en aumento."

65. *OC* omits from the stage direction from "Lleva peluca" until "velo." Note that "con cierto embarazo" may refer to being pregnant[*embarazada*].

66. *OC* and *LO* have "la plata." In the manuscript, it can be seen that when this same verse is repeated at the end of the MANIQUI's third speech, Lorca crossed out the word "plata" and chose "ropa."

67. *OC* has "llevará."

68. *OC* has "boca."

69. In the manuscript, there are two speeches that were replaced in *CA*: "MANIQUI. – ¿Por qué no viniste? JOVEN. – ¡Deja!"

70. *OC* and *LO* have "Las fuentes." In the manuscript, "pechos" is crossed out.

71. *OC* and *LO* have "abeja."

72. *OC* and *LO* omit the stage direction "*[Coge el trajecito]*."

73. *OC* and *LO* end the question at "llega," the same as in the next question of the JOVEN.

74. *OC* and *LO* have "la mujer."

75. In the manuscript there follow two crossed-out verses that read: "con una rosa en el vientre muerta, de blanca locura."

76. *OC* and *LO* have "su vientre." The preceding note clarifies our "en."

77. *OC* and *LO* omit the stage direction "*[Por el traje del niño]*."

78. "NO" is in capital letters in the manuscript.

79. *OC* and *LO* have "tus."

80. *LO* has "natural."

81. *OC* and *LO* have "en que entra."

82. What follows up until "lo pasado, pasado" in the VIEJO's speech, appears to have been cut in *CA*; nevertheless, we believe the speech ought to be reinstated.

83. *OC* and *LO* have "Tiene."

84. *OC* and *LO* omit from the stage direction "por un balcón."

85. *OC* and *LO* omit from the stage direction "Acercándose."

86. Here ends the cut made in *CA*, with which we disagree. See above, Note 82.

87. *OC* and *LO* omit the stage direction "*[Severo]*."

88. *OC* and *LO* add "¡Espera!" one more time, and the stage direction that follows reads, "*[Sale. Sus voces se pierden.]*"

89. In the manuscript occurs the following: "La CRIADA entra rápidamente, coge el candelabro y sale por el balcón. CRIADA. – ¡Ay la señorita! ¡Dios mío! ¡La señorita! *[Sale la señorita con el jugador y el jugador con la señorita] [Se oye lejano el cláxon.]*" This speech of the CRIADA appears to have been cut in *CA*. *OC* and *LO* include it, cutting "*[Sale la señorita con el . . . con la señorita]*."

90. *OC* and *LO* omit all of this stage direction from "Queda la escena azul" to "muy lejana."

91. *CA* has "LAS 4 VOCES LEJANAS Y CONCERTADAS. – ¡Espera!" We believe that this refers to the voices of the PADRE and the VIEJO.

Act Three

1. *OC* and *LO* add "CUADRO PRIMERO."

2. *OC* and *LO* have "una escalerilla."

3. *OC* and *LO* have "plástico."

4. *LO* omits "cruza."

5. *LO* omits the six verses from "Y si el sueño" until "levanta!."

6. *OC* and *LO* have "con medidos intervalos más lejanos."

7. *LO* has "diría."

8. *OC* and *LO* have this verse as belonging to the ARLEQUIN.

9. *OC* and *LO* omit the stage direction "*[En voz baja]*."

10. *LO* has "lo mandan al mar."

11. *OC* and *LO* have this verse as belonging to the ARLEQUIN.

12. *OC* and *LO* substitute this stage direction for "*[Al público]*." We have translated both, since one seems to clarify the other.

13. This speech has been added in *OC* and *CA*.

14. *OC* and *LO* add in this stage direction, "Lleva el compás con la cabeza."

15. *OC* and *LO* omit this speech and make the stage direction that goes with it into part of the previous one.

16. *OC* omits the stage direction "*[Canta]*" and makes this speech belong to the ARLEQUIN. *LO* has "¿No ves donde está?"

17. In the manuscript the following two verses are crossed out: "Segando las algas/del fondo del mar."

18. *OC* and *LO* omit from the stage direction "gritando."

19. *OC* has "*[ARLEQUIN ríe]*."

20. *OC* continues, "Luego nos iremos/al agua del mar." In the manuscript, these verses clearly belong to next speech of the MUCHACHA.

21. *OC* and *LO* omit from the stage direction "y volviéndose."

22. *OC* puts this stage direction before "Verdad." and makes the two following verses into part of the previous speech of the MUCHACHA. See above, Note 20.

23. *OC* and *LO* omit the stage direction "*[Levemente incrédulo]*."

24. *LO* omits the four verses from "Perdí rosa" until "encontrar."

25. *OC* and *LO* omit from the stage direction "a voces."

26. *LO* has this speech as belonging to the PAYASO.

27. *OC* and *LO* place this stage direction after "PAYASO. – un vals."

28. *LO* has "*[En alta voz]*."

29. *OC* and *LO* have "de nubes."

30. *OC* and *LO* omit from the stage direction "de una sola gasa."

31. *OC* and *LO* have "traje 1900 con larga cola amarillo rabioso."

32. *OC* and *LO* omit from the stage direction "de tetas altas ha de estar."

33. *OC* and *LO* have "portera."

34. *OC* and *LO* omit "Yo crucé la biblioteca y ." Note that the following dialogue is exactly the same as that in the first act between the MECANOGRAFA and the JOVEN, only that here the speakers are reversed. Likewise, the MASCARA is the mother of the NIÑO MUERTO, whose crying could be heard.

35. *OC* has "en pie."

36. *OC* and *LO* have "señorita." Note that in the first stage direction of this scene, it is said that the MASCARA "habla con un leve acento italiano." These and the other Italianisms of the character are in *CA*.

37. *OC* and *LO* have "¿Por qué, señorita?"

38. *OC* and *LO* have "dulcísimo tormento, amiga mía."

39. *OC* and *LO* add "he."

40. *OC* and *LO* omit "así."

41. *OC* and *LO* have "amigo."

42. *OC* and *LO* omit "Nunca es enseguida." In the manuscript, after the question "¿Y cuándo llega tu amigo?" the following has been

crossed out: "MECANOGRAFA. – Enseguida. MASCARA. –*[Son-riendo]* ¡O sea nunca! MECANOGRAFA. – ¡Claro!" The phrase "Nunca es enseguida," however, is not crossed out.

43. In the manuscript the word "llegará" is crossed out and replaced with the word "tardará." This same word is the one with which Lorca replaced that word "enseguida" in the MECANOGRAFA's first reply, cited in the previous note.

44. *OC* and *LO* have "¿Por qué? ¿Por qué?"

45. *OC* and *LO* have "seguro."

46. *OC* and *LO* puts from "tan alto" through "especial" between dashes.

47. *OC* and *LO* have "amiga."

48. *LO* has "Viste un traje de campo con medias."

49. *OC* has "¿Han cerrado el paseo?" *LO* has "¿Han cerrado el paso?"

50. Added in *OC* and *CA*.

51. *OC* and *LO* omit the stage direction "*[Estremecido]*."

52. This entire speech of the ARLEQUIN seems to have been cut in *CA*, but we have included it, because we believe it improves the clarity of the passage.

53. *OC* and *LO* omit the stage direction "*[No queriendo oir]*."

54. *OC* and *LO* have "Iniciando."

55. *OC* and *LO* omit "¡Ayy!"

56. Added in *CA*. *OC* has "Busca."

57. Added in *CA*.

58. *OC* and *LO* omit from the stage direction "El PAYASO le hace señas."

59. *OC* and *LO* have "marcando un paso de baile y con el dedo sobre los labios."

60. *OC* and *LO* omit the stage direction "*[Las luces del teatro se encienden]*."

61. *OC* and *LO* omit from the stage direction "*[llena de júbilo]*."

62. *OC* and *LO* omit the stage direction "*[Abrazándola]*."

63. *OC* and *LO* omit the stage direction "*[Abrazándolo]*." In the manuscript, the following is crossed out:
"Ahora sé que me quieres
que siempre me has querido."

64. *LO* has "guardan."

65. *OC* omits "en."

66. *OC* and *LO* have "tus brazos."

67. *LO* omits "harta."
68. *LO* omits "cubrir."
69. *OC* and *LO* have "Un ruiseñor que canta."
70. *OC* and *LO* have "aire."
71. *OC* omits this verse.
72. *OC* has "tan lejos."
73. *OC* and *LO* omit the last "siempre."
74. *OC* and *LO* omit the stage direction "*[Enérgico y con pasión]*."
75. *OC, LO, AU* AND *CA* have "*[Se deshace del JOVEN]*." The correction is ours.
76. We add this verse because this is otherwise the same strophe that has appeared on two previous occasions in this same scene. We believe that here it was left out inadvertently.
77. *OC* and *LO* have "teatro."
78. *OC* has "tonos pálidos." *LO* has "tomos."
79. *OC* has "escena."
80. *OC* and *LO* omit from the stage direction "mientras llora."
81. *OC* has "*[en voz baja]*."
82. *OC* and *LO* have "¡No quiero!"
83. *OC* and *LO* add "venir."
84. *OC* and *LO* have "a subir lentamente la escalera."
85. *LO* has "Ven."
86. *OC* and *LO* omit "viva" and have " y observa lentamente."
87. *OC* omits "en."
88. *OC* has "hormiga."
89. *OC* and *LO* have "MASCARA AMARILLA."
90. In *CA*, the following stage direction is added: "*[Aquí marcándose unos pasos de can-can.]*"
91. *LO* has "notar."
92. In the manuscript, the word "treinta" is crossed out.
93. *OC* and *LO* have "rosas."
94. The word "Espera." is added in both *OC* and *CA*.
95. "NO" is in capital letters in the manuscript.
96. *OC* and *LO* omit the stage direction "*[Abrazándolo]*."
97. *OC* and *LO* have "una cortina y el ARLEQUIN un violín blanco."

98. *OC* and *LO* put the speech "¿Queda atrás?" in the mouth of the ARLEQUIN. In the manuscript, it can be seen that although this was Lorca's first idea, the word "ARLEQUIN" is crossed out and written anew at the beginning of the following speech:
"ARLEQUIN. – La mortaja del aire.
PAYASO. – Y la musica de tu violín."

99. *OC* and *LO* have this speech in the mouth of the PAYASO. See above, Note 98.

100. Added in *CA*. In the manuscript, the two following speeches are crossed out:
"MASCARA. – El conde besa mi retrato de amazona.
VIEJO. – Vamos a no llegar pero vamos a ir."

101. *OC* adds here "Me iré contigo." as the JOVEN's speech, when this phrase belongs, as we have just seen, to the MECANOGRAFA and was added in *CA*. Note once again the possible double meaning of the verb "irse," as a parallel to the erotic scene at the beginning of Act Two between the NOVIA and the JUGADOR DE RUGBY.

102. *OC* and *LO* have "la mano."

103. *OC* has "Quedan." This is a repetition of the previous strophe of the ARLEQUIN and PAYASO, whose speeches are correctly placed this time in *OC* and *LO*. See above, Note 98.

104. *OC* and *LO* have "MASCARA." These two speeches are the ones that were previously crossed out in the manuscript. See above, Note 100.

105. *OC* and *LO* don't correctly indicate its position as completion of the verse.

106. We believe that the two "¡Por allí!" are meant to be said simultaneously, and that for this reason are put in the same position as twin completions of the verse.

107. We have cut the speech that continued "ARLEQUIN. –*[Irónico]* ¡Por allí!" It is superfluous and breaks the verse.

Act Three
Final Scene

1. *OC* and *LO* have "CUADRO SEGUNDO."

2. In the manuscript, the following is crossed out: "A la derecha hay tres señores jugando a los naipes." As can be seen, this later became, "A la derecha una mesa."

3. In the manuscript the word "Estuvo" is crossed out.

4. Note the confusion that Lorca imparts to the scene by the inconsistent use of "sale" in the stage directions. Here, it indicates that the character is leaving the stage, but in the first stage direction of this scene, the phrase "Sale el CRIADO . . . " means that he is entering the stage.

5. *OC* and *LO* have "muestras de desesperanza y desfallecimiento físico."

6. In the manuscript, the word "pequeño" is crossed out.

7. *OC* and *LO* have "a los veinte años."

8. *OC* and *LO* omit the stage direction "*[Sonriente]*."

9. In the manuscript, "Sí." is crossed out in this speech. Likewise, the phrase "Lo celebro in" in the following speech of the CRIADO is crossed out. Lorca situated the phrases several lines below.

10. *OC* and *LO* omit the stage direction "*[Bebe]*."

11. Note that this indicates the JOVEN is still wearing his blue pajamas, as he was at the beginning of the play.

12. *OC* and *LO* change the stage direction "*[Irritado]*" into "*[Excitado]*."

13. In the manuscript, the words "el lecho" are crossed out.

14. *OC* and *LO* omit the stage direction "*[Alegre]*."

15. In the manuscript, the following is crossed out: "Me la regaló mi madre."

16. *OC* omits from the stage direction "Pausa."

17. *OC* and *LO* have "cinta."

18. *LO* has "Sí."

19. *LO* has "brota."

20. *OC* and *LO* have "abrigo."

21. *OC* and *LO* have "la."

22. *OC* and *LO* have "¡Ah!"

23. In the manuscript, "forradas de raso blanco" is crossed out.

24. *LO* gives this speech to the JOVEN, an obvious impossibility.

25. *OC* and *LO* omit "en dos chorros."

26. *OC* and *LO* have "de azul."

27. *LO* has "Jalaraja."

28. *OC* and *LO* give this speech to JUGADOR 2, but in the manuscript, it is clearly given to JUGADOR 1.

29. "Otra" is double-underlined in the manuscript.

30. *OC* and *LO* give this speech to JUGADOR 2, a change forced on them by having given the previous speech to JUGADOR 3. See above, Note 28.

31. *OC* and *LO* omit the stage direction "*[Riendo]*."

32. *OC* and *LO* omit "¡Cá!" *OC* has "Yo guardo," and *LO* has "Yo pongo."

33. *OC* and *LO* give this speech to JUGADOR 2, though in the manuscript, it is clearly given to JUGADOR 3.

34. *OC* and *LO* have "*[En broma]*."

35. *OC* has "se clava."

36. *OC* and *LO* omit the stage direction "*[Riendo]*."

37. In the manuscript, the word "nunca" is crossed out.

38. *LO* has "nunca más."

39. *OC* and *LO* add "en."

40. *OC* gives this speech to JUGADOR 3, though in the manuscript it is clearly given to JUGADOR 1.

41. *OC* and *LO* omit the "y" in the stage direction, changing the sense of the phrase, which now reads, "*[Se las da a los demás.]*"

42. *OC* and *LO* drop the stage direction "*[Con voz grave]*" in favor of "*[En voz baja]*."

43. Added in *OC* and *CA*. Nevertheless, in *OC*, the stage direction is placed before the two sentences. We have followed the placement as in *CA*.

44. The same case as in the previous speech. *OC* and *LO* omit from the stage direction the word "y."

45. *OC* and *LO* have "Yo juego." In the manuscript, it is clearly written, "¡Y juego!" Thereafter, in the following stage direction, the word "las" is crossed out and replaced with "una," and the plural is changed into the singular "carta."

46. *OC* has "*[Excitado con una carta]*." This stage direction ought to be written with a comma, since otherwise the meaning changes. In fact, Lorca wrote it as follows, in the manuscript: "*[Excitado] [Con una carta]*."

47. *OC* and *LO* have "sus."

48. *OC* has "las." As will be seen, the reference is to a single card.

49. *OC* and *LO* add a comma: "¿Cómo, no hay whisky?," changing the sense.

50. *OC* and *LO* have "La carta."

51. *OC* has "algas." *LO* has "cabras." *AU* also has "cabras." We interpreted Lorca's handwriting as "calzas," a guess that was confirmed on our examination of *CA*.

52. *OC* and *LO* omit "gran."

53. *OC* and *LO* add "de coeur."

54. *OC* and *LO* have "Hay que huir." In the manuscript, it is clearly written "¡Hay que vivir!," which, as can be seen, is the last thing that JUGADOR 3 says before leaving the stage.

55. This speech is added in *CA*. *OC* adds only "JUGADOR 3, – No hay que esperar." It also puts the phrase "Hay que vivir." in the following speech of the JOVEN: "JOVEN. – Juan, Juan. Hay que vivir . . ." And it omits the stage direction "*[Salen]*."

56. *OC* adds mistakenly "Hay que vivir."

57. *LO* has "Mi amor."

58. In *CA*, this stage direction is placed after "JOVEN. –Juan.," and it reads "*[Muere en el sofá]*."

59. The text in *CA* ends with the speech, "ECO. – Juan." and the final stage direction of the work, "*[Aparece el CRIADO con un candelabro encendido. En el reloj dan las doce. TELÓN.]*" The six speeches that had once been inserted between them were cut by Lorca in the rehearsals of the work with *CA*. *OC*, *LO* and *AU* all include the cut text, which is as follows:
"JOVEN. – ¿No hay . . . ?
ECO. – No hay . . .
SEGUNDO ECO. – *[Más lejano]* No hay . . .
JOVEN. – . . . ¿Ningún hombre aquí?
ECO. –Aquí . . .
SEGUNDO ECO. – Aquí . . .
[El JOVEN muere.]"

60. Place and date as they are written on the final page of manuscript beneath the word "–Telón–."

Buster Keaton's Outing

1. This line is added in the Losada edition.

2. The stage direction is added in the Losada edition.

The Maiden, the Sailor and the Student

1. The word "azul" is added in the Losada edition.

Chimera

1. Note that in Spanish, the word "chimera" also means "quarrel."
2. Both Aguilar and Losada editions agree on this reading, but, in our opinion, it should read, " . . . y si te enteras, tienes miedo." The whole sentence, then, would translate: "If you are not afraid, you don't realize it, and if you do realize it, you're afraid."

Trip to the Moon

1. From this point forward, there are two alternative systems for the enumeration of shots in the film. We have followed the preferred enumeration in the edition of Marie Laffranque (Loubressac: Braad Editions, 1980).

Check Out Receipt

Main Library
510-747-7777

Saturday, April 15, 2017 4:46:36 PM
26304

Item: 33341001088151
Title: Once five years pass and other
dramatic works
Material: Books
Due: 05/06/2017

Total items: 1

Thank You!

Appendix 1

Half-Open Legend

There is a white restlessness of storm
And a purple echo in everything.
The countryside is still. The city quiets
On this June afternoon tense and warm.

In my soul some vague legend stirs
Proud Pecopin and his night of a hundred years
And the priceless talisman the flood steals
And the laughter of the blackbird in the calm beech
And the shout of the devil who's laughing too.

One hundred years—Oh my God!—
Passed in that night of hunting and feasting
And the bird of love died in the castle
Though the blue remains forever calm
And Pecopin now aged understands the refrain
Of the blind birds that were crying: "Baldour!"
But their love was now impossible for the years
Had put out the light of their souls.

Oh, sad sad legend that the great Hugo tells us
Seated dreaming by the banks of the Rhine.
The horse of time doesn't stop though we
Grab tight to her mane with a hand of iron.

We hold a cup of gold in our hands
Full of a rare liquor that slowly spills
Each drop is a year that goes from the hoard
And in a single day we lose this cup of gold
For love that is fire can change it to flame
Or the hurt heart spills it all over.

Today I think of the legend
And deeply I shudder

I am young and the race is run before one knows it
I am sick with a love
And dying of the absence
Of a pair of divine lips that I might kiss.

Maybe my whole cup will spill in a night
And I have no castle, no talisman
The flood of the tale took it away forever
And the heart now aged only thinks to cry.
....
This afternoon is restless with a storm
And I with a legend to ponder.

6 June 1918

Leyenda a medio abrir

Hay una blanca inquietud de tormenta
Y un eco morado en todas las cosas.
El campo está quieto. La ciudad se calla
Esta tarde de junio sentida y bochornosa.

En mi alma se agita una vaga leyenda
La noche de cien años del bello Pécopin
Y el talismán precioso que el torrente se lleva
Y las risas del mirlo en el haya serena
Y el grito del diablo que se ríe también.

Cien años. ¡Ay, Dios mío!
Duró la noche aquella de caza y de festín
Y el ave del amor se murió en el castillo
Aunque siempre sereno continúa el azul
Y Pécopin ya viejo entiende el estribillo.
De los pájaros ciegos que gritaban: "¡Baldour!"
Pero era ya imposible el amor que los años
Habían apagado de sus almas la luz.

¡Oh, leyenda tristísima que el gran Hugo nos cuenta
Cuando estuvo soñando por la orilla del Rhin.
El caballo del tiempo no para aunque tengamos
Una mano de hierro sujetando su crin.

Una copa de oro tenemos en la mano
Llena de un licor raro que lento se derrama
Cada gota es un año que se va del tesoro

Y en un día perdemos esta copa de oro
Pues el amor que es fuego puede cambiarlo en llama
O el corazón doliente lo derrama del todo.

Hoy pienso en la leyenda
Y grave me estremezco
Soy joven y la senda se pasa sin pensar
De un amor adolezco
Y la ausencia me mata
De unos labios divinos donde poder besar.

Acaso en una noche se derrame mi copa
Y no tengo castillo ni tengo talismán
El torrente del cuento lo arrastró para siempre
Y el corazón ya viejo sólo piensa en llorar.
....

Tiene esta tarde inquietud de tormenta
Y yo una leyenda para meditar.

6 de junio de 1918

«Agua sexual»

Sexual Water

Appendix 2

In the Forest of the Grapefruits of Moon

Ecstatic Poem

Prologue

I am going on a long trip.

On a silver mirror, much before the sun comes up, I find the suitcase and the clothes that I will need for the wholly strange lands and the theoretical gardens.

Poor and quiet, I wish to visit the ecstatic world where all my possibilities and lost landscapes live. I wish to enter cold but sharp into the garden of the unblossomed seed and of the blind theories, in search of the love that I never had but that was mine.

I spent long days looking through all the mirrors in my house to find the road that leads to that wonderful garden, and at last— purely by chance!—I found it.

I tried any number of procedures. For example, I began to sing in such a way that my voice hung long and tense in the air, but the mirrors remained silent. I executed complex geometries in word and rhythm, I filled the eyes with silver by my wail, and I even put a shade on the little lamp that lights the grotto of my head, but it was all useless!

One veiled morning, after I'd given up the idea of the trip as impossible and had found myself free of worries and invisible gardens, I went to comb my hair in front of a mirror and, without my asking anything, its broad silver face filled up with a zigzag of nightingale song, and from the depths of the quicksilver arose the clear and the precise key, a key that naturally I am forbidden to reveal.

I calmly set out on this trip and of course I wash my hands, I will tell what I see, but don't ask me to explain anything.

I might have gone to the country of the dead but I prefer to go to the country of what is not alive, which is not at all the same thing.

Of course a *pure and fulfilled* soul would not feel this curiosity. I go calmly. In the suitcase, I carry a good supply of fireflies.

○ ● ○

Before leaving I feel a sharp pain in my heart. My family's asleep and the whole house rests in absolute repose. The dawn revealing towers and counting one by one the leaves of the trees dresses me in a white mask and gloves of [....................]

End of Prologue

En el Bosque de las Toronjas de Luna

Poema extático

Prólogo

Me voy a un largo viaje.

Sobre un espejo de plata encuentro, mucho antes de que amanezca, el maletín y la ropa que debo usar por las extrañísimas tierras y jardines teóricos.

Pobre y tranquilo, quiero visitar el mundo extático donde viven todas mis posibilidades y paisajes perdidos.

Quiero entrar frío pero agudo en el jardín de las simientes no florecidas y de las teorías ciegas, en busca del amor que no tuve pero que era mío.

He buscado durante largos días por todos los espejos de mi casa el camino que conduce a ese jardín maravilloso y al fin ¡por pura casualidad! lo he encontrado.

Adopté muchos procedimientos. Por ejemplo, me puse a cantar procurando que mi voz se mantuviera larga y tensa sobre el aire, pero los espejos permanecían silenciosos. Hice complicadas geometrías con la palabra y el ritmo, llené los ojos de plata con mi llanto y hasta puse una pantalla a la lamparita que ilumina la gruta de mi cabeza ¡pero todo fue inútil!

Una mañana velada, después que había desechado por imposible el proyecto de viaje y me hallaba libre de preocupaciones y de jardines invisibles, fui a peinarme ante un espejo y, sin preguntarle nada, su ancha cara de plata se llenó de un zigzag de cantos de ruiseñores, y en la profundidad del azogue surgió la clave clara y precisa, clave que naturalmente me está vedado revelar.

Yo emprendo sereno este viaje y desde luego me lavo las manos, contaré lo que vea, pero no me pidáis que explique nada.

Pude haber ido al país de los muertos pero prefiero ir al país de lo que no vive, que no es lo mismo.

Desde luego que un alma *pura y completa* no sentiría esta curiosidad. Voy tranquilo. En el maletín llevo una buena provisión de luciérnagas.

○ ● ○

Antes de marchar siento un dolor agudo en el corazón. Mi familia duerme y toda la casa está en un reposo absoluto. El alba revelando torres y contando una a una las hojas de los árboles me pone un antifaz blanco y unos guantes de [..................]

Fin de Prólogo

Marinero [h. 1934–1936]

Sailor

Bibliography

(*For a list of editions of* Así que pasen cinco años, see Notes.)

Auclair, Marcelle. *Enfances et mort de Federico García Lorca*. Paris: Editions du Seuil, 1968.

Cao, Antonio F. *Federico García Lorca y las vanguardias: hacia el teatro*. London: Tamesis Books, 1984.

García Lorca, Federico. *Conferencias*. 2 volumes. Madrid: Alianza Editorial, 1984.

———. *Deep Song and Other Prose*. Edited and translated by Christopher Maurer. New York: New Directions, 1975.

———. "Escribe a su familia desde Nueva York y La Habana," *Poesía, Revista ilustrada de información poética*, 23–24. Edited by Christopher Maurer. Madrid: Ministerio de Cultura, 1986.

———. *Epistolario*. 2 volumes. Madrid: Alianza Editorial, 1983.

———. *El público y Comedia sin título*. Barcelona: Editorial Seix Barral, 1978.

———. *Suites*. Edited by Andre Belamich. Barcelona: Editorial Ariel, 1983.

García Lorca, Francisco. *Federico y su mundo*. Madrid: Alianza Editorial, 1980.

———. *In the Green Morning, Memories of Federico*. Translated by Christopher Maurer. New York: New Directions, 1986.

García-Posada, Miguel. *García Lorca*. Madrid: Edaf, 1979.

Gibson, Ian. *Federico García Lorca*. 2 volumes. Barcelona: Ediciones Grijalbo, 1985.

Huélamo Kosma, Julio. *Claves interpretativas de "Así que pasen cinco años"*. Memoria de Licenciatura, Madrid, 1981.

Laffranque, Marie. *Les idees esthetiques de Federico García Lorca*. Paris: Centre de Recherches Hispaniques, 1967.

Londre, Felicia Hardison. *Federico García Lorca*. New York: Frederick Unger Publishing Co., 1984.

Martín, Eutimio. *Federico García Lorca, heterodoxo y mártir*. Madrid: Siglo XXI de España Editores, 1986.

Martínez Nadal, Rafael. *El público: amor y muerte en la obra de Federico García Lorca*. Mexico City: Joaquín Mortiz, 1970.

Morris, C. B. *Surrealism and Spain*. London: Cambridge University Press, 1972.

Biographical Note

About the Playwright

FEDERICO GARCÍA LORCA (*1898–1936*) is the leading Spanish playwright and poet of the twentieth century. His twelve major works for the theatre have been produced around the world. They are *El maleficio de la mariposa* (*The Butterfly's Evil Spell*), 1919, *Mariana Pineda*, 1925, *Los títeres de cachiporra* (*The Billyclub Puppets*), 1928, *La zapatera prodigiosa* (*The Shoemaker's Prodigious Wife*), 1930, *Amor de Don Perlimplín con Belisa en su jardín* (*Don Perlimplín*), 1931, *Retablillo de Don Cristóbal* (*The Frame of Don Cristóbal*), 1931, *Así que pasen cinco años* (*Once Five Years Pass*), 1931, *El público* (*The Audience*), 1933, *Bodas de sangre* (*Blood Wedding*), 1933, *Yerma*, 1934, *Doña Rosita la soltera* (*Doña Rosita the Spinster*), 1935, and *La casa de Bernarda Alba* (*The House of Bernarda Alba*), 1936.

About the Translators

WILLIAM BRYANT LOGAN received a National Endowment for the Humanities grant in 1983 to translate three plays by Pedro Calderón de la Barca. He has published numerous translations of Lorca's poems and has completed a version of *Poet in New York*. He works in New York, writing poems, nonfiction, stories, and journalism. He and Gil are currently translating Ramón del Valle Inclán's *Comedias Bárbaras*.

ANGEL GIL ORRIOS is a director, writer, designer, and teacher. He has directed more than forty productions, including Lorca's *The House of Bernarda Alba, The Audience* and *Play Without a Title*. His many awards include the 1987 Silver Medal of the Académie des Arts-Sciences-Lettres in Paris, and the 1989 ACE Award for Best Director by the Association of Hispanic Critics of New York. He has been working on a stage concept for *Once Five Years Pass* since 1974.

•

CHRISTOPHER MAURER is Associate Professor of Languages and Literatures at Harvard University, editor of *Poetical Works of Federico García Lorca* (Farrar, Straus, and Giroux), and author of numerous studies and translations of Lorca's work.